OUR HOLLOW EARTH

An Inner World Paradise, Or a Gateway To Hell?

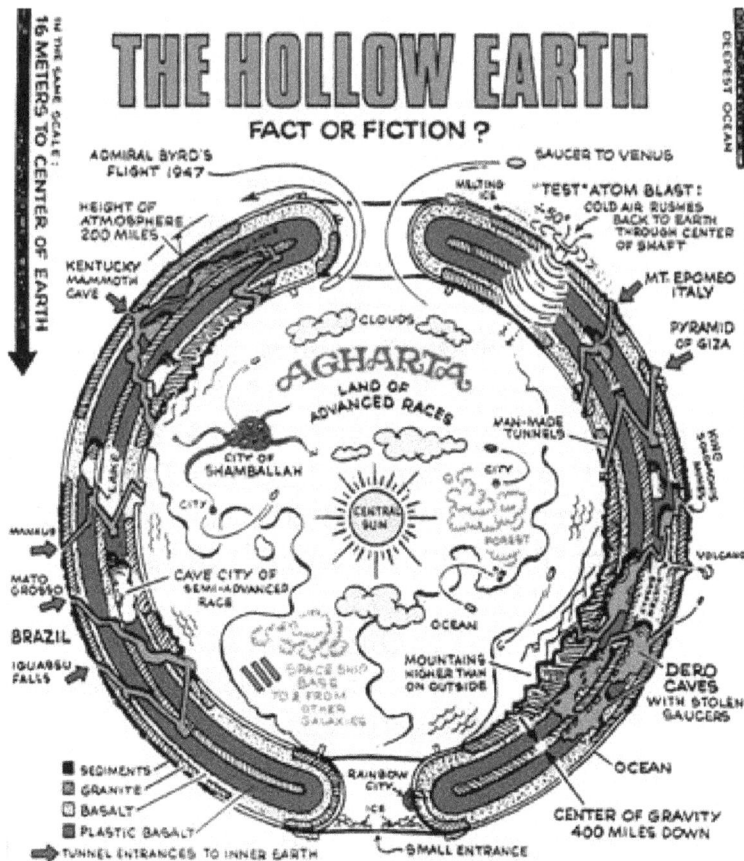

THE HOLLOW EARTH

FACT OR FICTION ?

i

OUR HOLLOW EARTH
An Inner World Paradise, Or a Gateway To Hell?
Timothy Green Beckley, Sean Casteel, Tim R. Swartz, Scott Corrales, Paul Dale Roberts, Deanna Jaxine Stinson, Hercules Invictus, Tim Cridland, Ludvig Holberg

Published in the United States of America By
Global Communications/Conspiracy Journal
Box 753 · New Brunswick, NJ 08903

Staff Members
Timothy G. Beckley, Publisher
Carol Ann Rodriguez, Assistant to the Publisher
Sean Casteel, General Associate Editor
Tim R. Swartz, Graphics and Editorial Consultant
William Kern, Editorial and Art Consultant

Sign Up On The Web For Our Free Weekly Newsletter
and Mail Order Version of Conspiracy Journal
and Bizarre Bazaar
www.ConspiracyJournal.com

Order Hot Line: 1-732-602-3407
PayPal: MrUFO8@hotmail.com

CONTENTS

Chapter One...1
IS PARADISE TO BE FOUND INSIDE THE EARTH?
OR IS THE SUBTERRANEAN WORLD AN ENTRANCEWAY TO HELL?
By Timothy Green Beckley

Chapter Two...7
THE PRIVATE HELL OF RICHARD SHAVER
AND THE COMING OF THE FLYING SAUCERS
By Sean Casteel

Chapter Three...15
HAS THE MYSTERIOUS HOLE
AT THE POLE BEEN PHOTOGRAPHED?
By Tim Cridland

Chapter Four...21
TIM R. SWARTZ: THE HOLLOW EARTH TOURIST
By Sean Casteel

Chapter Five...39
THE RIVER WILL GUIDE YOU HOME
By Deanna Jaxine Stinson
RIVERS OF THE UNDERWORLD -
A HALO PARANORMAL INVESTIGATION
By Paul Dale Roberts

Chapter Six...43
GIANTS IN THE EARTH:
THE OLYMPIANS, KINGS OF THE UNDERWORLD
An Olympian Exploration of Heaven and Hell
By Hercules Invictus

Chapter Seven...50
IS THERE A HOLLOW EARTH/JOHN F. KENNEDY
ASSASSINATION CONNECTION?
By Sean Casteel

Chapter Eight..60
SEARCHING FOR LATIN AMERICAN
ENTRANCES TO THE UNDERWORLD
By Scott Corrales

Chapter Nine...71
JOURNEY UNDER THE GROUND
By Ludvig Holberg

Conspiracy Journal
PRODUCTIONS

OUR HOLLOW EARTH

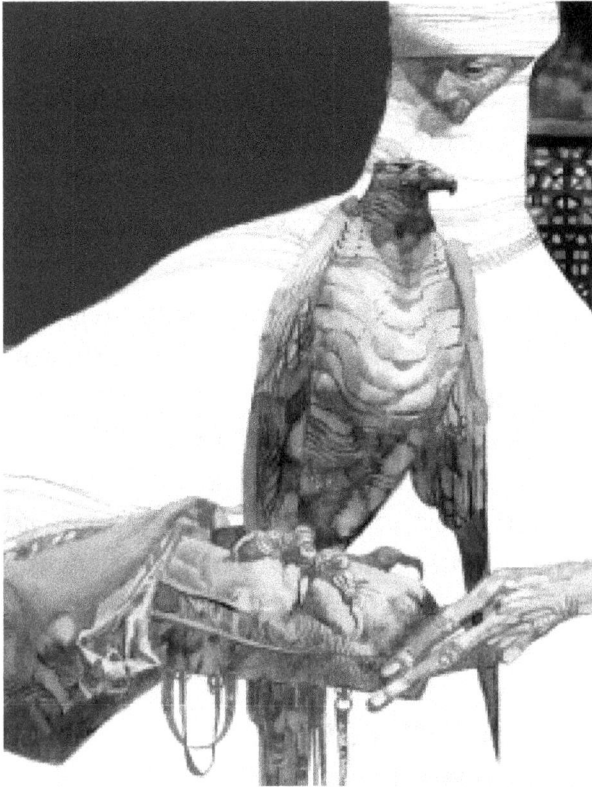

1 PRELUDE

IS PARADISE TO BE FOUND INSIDE THE EARTH?
OR IS THE SUBTERRANEAN WORLD AN ENTRANCEWAY TO HELL?
By Timothy Green Beckley

I have long been intrigued with the idea that our planet is a strange place in which to reside. You can bet your Slim Jim on that. For we might not even be "alone" here, as there could be "others" nearby who might really be in charge and are keeping their whereabouts unknown for a variety of reasons.

One of the reasons for this deep silence may be that the powers that be know that we are unsafe from monsters like Godzilla, who - it was revealed in the latest film franchise - lives beneath the Earth in catacombs and ventures up when some natural disaster or the testing of nuclear weapons jars him awake.

Frankly, the text books - the truth according to our "experts" - are all wrong! If you think life exists only on the surface of the planet, you have been listening to the "party line" way too long, for there are those who see the Earth as being multilayered, and that what goes on "above" definitely goes on "below" - and maybe more so to the extreme.

One of my mentors in the paranormal taught me this, when he took me on and allowed me to write a regular column, "On the Trail of the Flying Saucers," for his magazine "Flying Saucers From Other Worlds." The ETH theory was still the order of the day, but I was impressed by the words my editor/publisher was writing in editorials in the same publication where my feature regularly appeared.

Iconic publisher, editor, and offbeat author, the late Raymond Arthur Palmer, promoted some pretty curiously whacky - extreme - ideas during his life. Often said to be the man who "invented" the flying saucer mystery, RAP - as his fans in sci-fi fandom nicknamed him— started his brilliant, but controversial, career from an office in the Windy City by editing "Amazing Stories" magazine back in the

OUR HOLLOW EARTH

1930s. RAP became best known for publishing the wickedly profound tales of one Richard S. Shaver, who claimed he knew about a race of underground beings he called the Dero. For eons, the Dero had been polluting humankind's minds with murderous thoughts and were responsible for plagues, "natural" disasters, wars and all manner of evil deeds. They inflicted these woes upon humankind through the use of ancient laser-like "stim rays" shot forth from their cavernous dwellings, hidden out of sight below the very bottoms of our feet. .

Shaver said there was a real hell and it was located not in some mythical place but down below, right beneath us, toward the center of the earth. Like it or not, fundamentalist "scholars" tell us quite clearly that hell is for real and located inside the earth, making reference to Ephesians 4:9 which says of Jesus: "Now in saying that He ascended, what does it mean but that He also descended into the LOWER PARTS OF THE EARTH?" This, we are led to believe, is backed up on page 85 of a book by Dr. Rawlings, when the MD says that patients who died and were thrown into the fiery lakes of hell said, "...this place seems to be UNDERGROUND or WITHIN THE EARTH in some way." Isn't Hell located inside the Earth somewhere in a fiery pit? So be it, oh Lord!

TRAVEL TO THE CENTER OF THE EARTH
AND FIND IT TEAMING WITH LIFE!

I remember back in the 1960s reading an ad that ran in just about every pulp magazine about a book by Dr. Raymond Bernard on how flying saucers were NOT from outer space but came from inside the Earth. It constituted a preposterous statement if there ever was one - or at least so I thought in my early teens. Truth is, the first book I wrote and had published by Gray Barker's Saucerian Press was a mighty tome that still remains in print in one form or another. "The Shaver Mystery and the Inner Earth," went into several printings and eventually evolved into "Subterranean Worlds Inside Earth," which has sold year after year, decade after decade, and has even been translated into Japanese and Korean.

Of course, stories about traveling to various locales inside the Earth are nothing new. Unlike Shaver's tales of the demonic Dero who inhabit a cavern world, the inhabitants of the actual hollow earth, located at the planet's core, are said to be peaceful in countenance but wish to keep their existence a secret for fear that the surface "warmongers" will want to invade. Everyone must have read Jules Verne's "Journey To The Center Of The Earth," so when we reprinted the long out-of-print edition and expanded upon the original version of "The Smokey God And Other Inner Earth Mysteries," frankly we realized there isn't anything new under the sun - even the central sun said to light the interior of our planet. Anyone who has read this gem of a book will realize its relevance to the subject of a hollow earth, of that I am certain!

The story of the Smoky God is dramatic and tells of a fantastic journey by fa-

OUR HOLLOW EARTH

ther and son to a place inhabited by gentle giants. And we even dared to include the article by Ray Palmer that broke the ice so to speak, offering evidence in an early issue of "Flying Saucers From Other Worlds" magazine that there are entrances to the Hollow Earth at the North and South Pole.

Unlike with a rather admittedly demented Richard Shaver, who made no effort to conceal his hearing voices inside his head, voices that drove him nearly insane (he is said to have been locked in an insane asylum for several years), most of the tales of a Hollow Earth are rather benign, although some who ventured down reportedly encountered a rocky descent fraught with nightmarish extinct monsters who persisted in blocking their path. No pain, no gain, is proven once again to be a truism I suppose you could say.

A simplistic synopsis notes all the perils that befall Verne's inner earth adventurers. "Written in 1864, Jules' work is a highly accredited science fiction novel, where the character Axel is separated from his uncle and guide; he despairs that he will die from hunger and thirst in the dark cavern. The travelers soon come to the shore of a vast underground sea. There they see huge mushrooms, which are identified as the giant champignons. In addition, there are more forms of fungi and bizarre plants. The explorers know that they have to cross a sea and do so, but this sea is much larger than they expect. On their watery route, they see a battle between massive, ancient creatures-the ichthyosaur and plesiosaur. As the journey continues, the weather shifts and a massive storm begins. The adventurers are tossed about on the waves; thunder and lightning sound and spark all around. An electric ball alights on the explorers' raft and flames burst out."

Verne's novel is often credited with being the first book to deal with the concept that the earth could possibly be hollow. But in actually it was written about a hundred years after the release of a book that purports to be a real account of the author's exploits in the underworld.

As far as is known, our translation of Niels Klim's "Underground Travels," originally published in Danish as "Nicolai Klimii Iter Subterraneum" (1741), is a purportedly real journey as described by the Norweigian author Ludvig Holberg. It is being published here in English without tampering or unneeded editing.

The work begins with a foreword that assures the reader that everything in the story is a real account of the title character's exploits in the Underworld. The story is set, according to the book, in the Norwegian harbor town of Bergen in 1664, after Klim returns from Copenhagen, where he has studied philosophy and theology at the University of Copenhagen and graduated magna cum laude. His curiosity drives him to investigate a strange cave in a mountainside above the town, which sends out regular gusts of warm air. He ends up falling down the hole, and after a while he finds himself floating in free space.

Some have said that Ludvig Holberg's prose surpasses that of Jules Verne, but that is a matter of individual taste.

Our own historical scribe, Sean Casteel, critically examined the manuscript while in the editing process and summarized the author's tale with a comparison to some of the more recent volumes on the inner and hollow earth mysteries, a topic that continues to be a popular theme both in movies and in literature. The number of adherents to the theory that UFOs originate inside the planet is immense and I found in my own publishing efforts that hollow earth books can be more popular than the extraterrestrial hypnosis, which would seem to be based on more of a solid scientific footing.

A SUMMATION OF NIELS KLIM'S HOLLOW EARTH JOURNEY
By Sean Casteel
COMPLETE TITLE: NIELS KLIM'S JOURNEY UNDER THE GROUND, BEING A NARRATIVE OF HIS WONDERFUL DESCENT TO THE SUBTERRANEAN LANDS, TOGETHER WITH AN ACCOUNT OF THE SENSIBLE ANIMALS AND TREES

The author is Ludvig Holberg, the most eminent writer among the Danes in the 18th century. University-educated and well-traveled, he wrote treatises on law as well as histories, satires and comedies.

"There are many persons of both sexes in my country who believe in fairies and supernatural beings and who are ready to swear that that they have been conveyed by spirits to hills and mountain caves," writes Holberg.

Klim, the hero of the tale, is likewise said to be transported to the world underground, where he meets with some "surprising" adventures. Many strange creatures inhabit this new world. Trees are introduced that have the power of speech and musical instruments discuss questions of philosophy and finance.

This introduction is followed by a short section called "Apologetic Preface," in which descendants of Klim the Great add a prefix to the new edition where they swear to the authenticity of the story and seek to amend the bad reputation with which the publisher has unfairly been burdened by readers who believe the book is all fantasy.

Some highlights from the book are summarized here.

Chapter One: The Author's Descent To The Abyss.

Having graduated from the university in Copenhagen, Denmark, Klim returned to his native Norway. He is prompted by academics in Norway as well as his own curiosity to explore a cave in the nearby mountains. He is "driven headlong through the air" and lands in another "globe," where he rambles for ten years before returning to his friends and native land.

After falling into the abyss for fifteen minutes, he encounters a faint light and soon after a clear and bright shining heaven. The sun, moon and stars looked much smaller than to the people on Earth, and he did not understand just where he was. He wondered if he had died and was about to be carried to the "blessed dwellings."

Then he realizes he must be in the subterranean firmament, saying there are those who insist that the Earth is hollow and that within its shell here is another lesser world, with corresponding sun, planets and stars.

Chapter Two: The Author's Arrival At The Planet Nazar.

Nazar is the name of the underground world, similar to Rampa's calling it Agharta. The author encounters the aforementioned speaking trees and will eventually learn to communicate with them. But first he is arrested by the underworld's sheriff on the charge that he had trifled with one of Nazar's females. He is tried in court and thrown in prison. Later, the sheriff, under orders from the king, sees to the author's learning the local language. In subsequent developments, the author is freed, having been falsely accused.

Chapter Five: The Kingdom of Potu and Its Inhabitants

"The whole planet - Nazar - is scarcely six hundred miles in circumference and may be traveled over its whole extent without guide or interpreter, for there is but one language throughout." The author says that Potu, part of Nazar, is the pinnacle of the inner planet in a way similar to Europe being the most developed portion of the surface world. (We realize this is no longer "politically correct.") The Potuans he encounters here are distinguished in the underground world for their virtue and understanding.

Chapter Six: The Religion of the Potuans.

"Whoever dares to dispute the being and nature of the Deity is sent to the madhouse and is bled. All agree in worshipping a superior being, whose omnipotence has created and whose providence maintains all things."

Chapter Nine:

After another brush with the law, this time a misunderstanding about the author's allegedly stolen coat, he is banished and made to return to the surface. He is exiled along with two others: a metaphysician who had made offensive remarks about spirits and a fanatic accused of seeking the overthrow of the world's religious and civil laws.

The author is placed in a large box with sufficient food for a few days. When the box is opened, he finds himself surrounded by a great multitude of monkeys, who spoke in a strange language and moved about with perfect dignity. He is taken to a large building where he is taught the language of the monkeys. This development is followed by pages of adventures and a love story involving an underground female.

He is later declared king of the underground world, having impressed the inhabitants with his heroism and leadership abilities.

OUR HOLLOW EARTH

At the story's end, the author finds himself at the same place where he had previously fallen into the cave. He wonders if the last ten years have been a dream, but realizes they haven't. But now he has fallen from being a king to being just another college graduate with a bachelor's degree. "I can never forget, for a moment," the author writes, "the splendor that once surrounded me."

To reiterate, this is all very similar to T. Lobsang Rampa's stories of the hidden world with a central sun and cities occupied by a beautiful and advanced people. It tells of an imperfect but basically benevolent society with laws and religious beliefs similar to ours on the surface. There is a magical element, however, with the talking trees and monkeys. Given that it was written in the 1700s, it's amazingly ahead of its time. And the writer does talk about belief in the underground world being a popular one in his era; it's interesting how this belief has carried on into our time.

OUR HOLLOW EARTH

**THE PRIVATE HELL OF
RICHARD SHAVER
AND THE COMING OF
THE FLYING SAUCERS**

By Sean Casteel

The Book of Ecclesiastes in the Old Testament decries repeatedly "the evil that is done under the sun," but what if there is also great evil done beneath the surface of the Earth? I have written previously about how flying saucers may originate from an Inner Earth paradise, but the late author and "victim" Richard Shaver would doubtless offer a vigorous protest to that idea.

For Shaver, as with most percipients of the paranormal, the strange experiences began in his childhood. In a book from Timothy Green Beckley's Global Communications/Inner Light Publications called "Richard Shaver: Reality of the Inner Earth," edited by Tim R. Swartz, Shaver describes hearing horrifying disembodied voices as a young boy.

"From as far back as I can remember," Shaver writes, "there were the voices. They weren't there all the time, but they were there enough that they played an important role in my early childhood development. At first I thought that everyone heard the voices. I thought there was nothing strange about being awakened at night with the hideous screams of someone being torn limb from limb ringing in your ears. I thought it was normal to hear the maniacal laughing of an invisible someone who thought it was a fine joke to see an innocent soul run down by a speeding train. I thought everyone knew that the voices were with us all of the time, watching, waiting, scheming for our bloody deaths. But I was wrong. It seemed that I was the only one who heard the voices. I learned quickly not to talk

7

about them, lest I be thought a maniac."

Shaver's voices gradually faded from his life and became only a distant childhood memory. They returned, however, when he was an adult working at an auto plant in Detroit. He began to hear them through the noise of the machinery, conversing among themselves about gleefully tearing the skin off a woman as she screamed for mercy or causing cars and planes to crash.

He concluded he must be quite insane, quit his job, began to live a hobo life and took to alcohol to try to block the voices out. He found himself confined to a prison or mental hospital - he seems unclear on which - and came to believe the voices came from people living in caves beneath the institution where he was incarcerated, tormenting him and the other prisoners with strange technologies he compared to some kind of x-rays.

Shaver writes: "My problems, I realized, did not stem from some kind of mental impairment. I wasn't crazy in the traditional sense, even though at times I felt like I was being driven mad by the hateful rays that were being beamed at me by the people below. No, I was sane in an insane world.

"I have often wondered," he continues, "how many people who have been institutionalized because they were diagnosed as crazy were in fact victims, such as myself, of the damnable rays. Did they themselves think that they were insane because of the voices they heard in their heads and voluntarily committed themselves? Even today I still wonder if most forms of mental illness are not actually insidious attacks from the world below."

Over time, perhaps as a method of coping with the voices, Shaver began to develop a myth or a narrative to explain them. He writes about the coming of the "Titans," a humanoid race that migrated from their home planet and settled on Earth long before mankind was created. The Titans created the first civilization on the Earth, a social and scientific utopia that has never been equaled since.

But there came a time when the sun began to flare in dangerous ways and Earth was flooded with world-destroying radiation. The Titans had no choice but to flee, but some of them stubbornly refused to abandon their homes and instead moved underground or beneath the seas. They took their great machines and scientific knowledge with them, in hopes of someday finding a solution to the solar radiation and returning to live on the Earth's surface.

But even deep within the Earth, the solar radiation continued to affect them. They tried moving deeper into the planet, but to no avail.

"Those who did not die immediately," Shaver writes, "suffered genetic damage that was passed down from generation to generation. Eventually, this once mighty race was reduced to mutated horrors, retarded in intelligence and social structure. Worse still, these monstrosities still had access to the self-repairing machines of their ancestors. But instead of using them for their intended purposes, they used them to satisfy their sick, twisted desires. These are the demons of ancient myth and folklore."

Shaver eventually began to write about this complex and bizarre scenario and sent a letter to a pulp sci-fi magazine called "Amazing Stories" in late 1943. At the time, the much-celebrated Ray Palmer was the editor, and he writes about discovering Shaver in another Global Communications release called "The Hidden World, Volume One," part of a series of books consisting of Shaver's collected writings.

"One day a letter came in," Palmer recalls, "giving the details of an 'ancient alphabet' that 'should not be lost to the world.' It was opened by my managing editor, Howard Browne, who read it with typical orthodox attitude and tossed it in the wastebasket with the comment, 'The world is full of crackpots.' Even through the intervening wall I heard his remark, and the word 'crackpot' drew me like a magnet."

Palmer began to experiment with the ancient alphabet, said to be the basis of all known human language, and realized the language system Shaver had written about actually worked. Palmer published the letter in "Amazing Stories," which quickly made pulp magazine publishing history. Hundreds of letters poured in asking where Shaver had gotten his alphabet. Shaver answered by submitting a 10,000 word manuscript, poorly typed and entitled "A Warning To Future Man."

Palmer read the manuscript through and then asked himself what it was he had exactly? It was not a simple matter of an author trying to make a sale. Shaver wanted no money for his manuscript, which was really more accurately a letter written as a warning. Shaver was anxious that it be published, not for notoriety but out of a sincere desire that the world be warned of the terrible danger it faced and informed of a wonderful heritage it had lost and which should be recovered if at all possible.

Palmer said the manuscript was problematic for "Amazing Stories." It was not a story about the future, based on factual science, the usual fare for the magazine. Shaver's manuscript instead purported to be about the science of the past. But Palmer saw that here was a "jumping off place" for some really terrific stories, and with his mind focused on potential profits for the magazine if the stories were properly packaged and promoted on the cover, he began to rewrite Shaver's manuscript into a longer story entitled "I Remember Lemuria." Palmer says he did not alter the "factual" basis of Shaver's manuscript but changed the story so that it did not revolve around literal caves in the Earth with actual people living there but instead was the product of "racial memory," a story encoded into Shaver's DNA from eons past. The point in doing this was to make it more believable to the magazine's readers, but the results went surprisingly beyond initial expectations.

Not only did readers find Shaver's story believable, they did so in unprecedented numbers. The issue of "Amazing Stories" that included "I Remember Lemuria" sold out its first press run of 135,000 copies, but this during World War II and even pulp paper was rationed by law. But through some shady dealing and with the help of Shaver's underground "contacts," sufficient paper was obtained to print another 50,000 copies, which sold out overnight. The enormous popularity of what came to be called the "Shaver Mysteries" had begun.

But that popularity did not come without some nay-saying. The readers of "Amazing Stories" were hardcore sci-fi buffs who weren't interested in some fantasy story that claimed to be true. They of course wrote to the magazine in protest. Meanwhile, one of the owners of the publishing company that included "Amazing Stories" in its empire of pulp magazines, Bernard Davis, called to say the extra 50,000 copies had been printed without the approval of higher ups and predicted they would not sell nor would the usual customers buy the first printing either. Of Shaver's story, Davis said, "I have never read such balderdash in my life."

Nevertheless, a total of around 50,000 people wrote letters praising "I Remember Lemuria," with many of them claiming to hear the same voices Shaver was hearing. Palmer writes of visiting Shaver at his home in Pennsylvania and reporting that he also heard voices as he lay in bed long after Shaver had retired for the night.

The complete text of "I Remember Lemuria" is reprinted in "The Hidden World, Volume One," and if you've never read it, it should go to the top of your "must-read" list. It's the one that started the whole ball rolling and is a classic work of occult lore. Historically, there are few things as significant to the entire field of Inner Earth belief.

Returning to Shaver's underground cosmology, the mutated, horrific creatures he described were given the name "dero," which is a combination of the words "detrimental" and "robot." Another variation is "degenerate robot." Shaver said we were all "deros" to some degree, descended from the same genetic stock, but that the actual underground dwellers took their evil to such extremes that there was virtually no comparison.

The dero not only caused wicked mayhem on the surface, such as wars and genocide and mass perversions and all forms of sadistic cruelty, it was also their primary pleasure, their reason for existence, their true joy in living. With their advanced technology, some of it capable of total mind control and even a kind of demonic possession, the dero were far more powerful than mankind's ability to resist and overcame our puny efforts at righteousness with a gleeful, supernatural ease.

This is of course a 20th century restatement of the age-old "Problem of Evil." Why, if God is our benevolent, loving Father, does evil exist with such a rigorous, insurmountable force? If we are made in God's image, why are we, collectively,

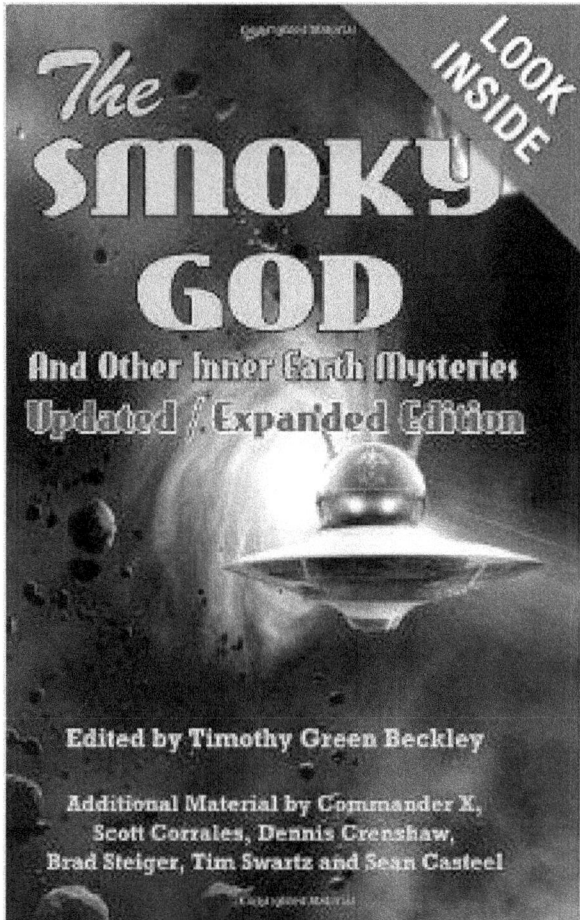

An historical account of a voyage to the cavern zone of the Inner Earth.

Hideous monsters of the dark cavern world, The Dero, menace the surface world.

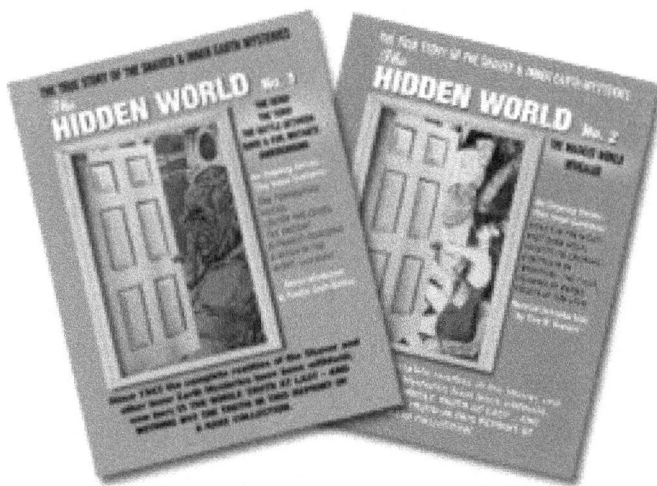

Covers from the fascinating "Hidden World" book series.

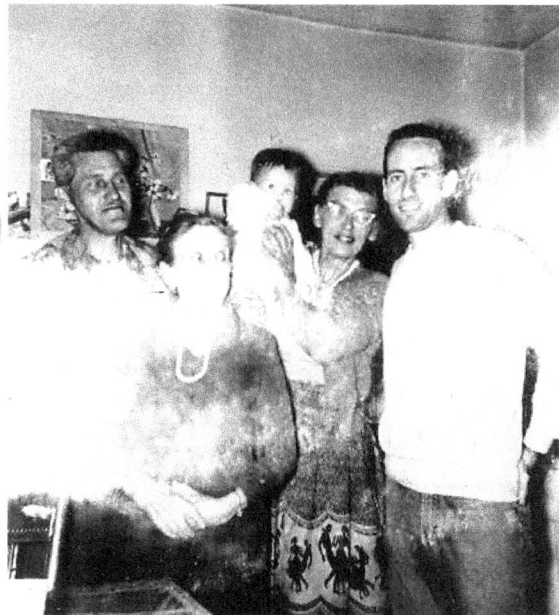

The late Richard Shaver in his Arkansas workplace with a group of admirers.

so screwed up? Shaver's answer, that the dero are to blame, seems as logical as any other attempt to explain the sorry state of the world. His dero are an acceptable variation on the theme of a deceiving Satan who caused mankind's fall from grace in Eden and has made war on us ever since. Shaver's monsters are also located in the hollows of the Earth itself, which is where hell is said to be located by believers in religion and mythology throughout the world and down through history.

Shaver successfully combined both ancient and familiar elements with a new modern urgency that was both original and very marketable, as the continued success reaped by Palmer and his publishing house bore witness to. Shaver began to write more stories about the dero in 1944 and had a long and profitable run with them. But the sci-fi buffs remained irate about the intrusion of nonfiction into their precious "Amazing Stories," and in 1948, in spite of the fact that he had built up the circulation to 200,000 a month, a figure unheard of for most pulp magazines of that era, Palmer decided to strike off on his own, having grown tired of the friction the situation was causing. That same year, Palmer teamed with Curtis Fuller and created "FATE Magazine," which is still being published today, more than 60 years later.

Global Communications/Inner Light Publications offers reprints of nearly all of Shaver's stories from that heady early period, both in "The Hidden World" series and another recent book called "Richard Shaver's Chilling Tales From The Inner Earth," edited by Timothy Green Beckley and William Kern. Also included are some of the original magazine covers, many of which look like quality "pop art" and would be worthy of an art museum or gallery showing.

By the early 1960s, the popularity of the Shaver Mysteries had essentially run its course and Shaver had moved on to something new. In his later years, Shaver had come to believe that ancient civilizations had used ordinary rocks to "capture their images."

"Just like you can put a lot of information on a computer disk today," explained publisher and writer Timothy Green Beckley, "Shaver believed that they encoded rocks with all kinds of legends and stories from the days of Atlantis and these underground worlds. He thought that everybody should be able to see the pictures and read the information in the rocks just like he was able to. So every week, he would send me a box of rocks through the mail or by UPS, containing all the dirt and worms and everything from his backyard."

In spite of the frequent rock shipments, which caused young Beckley's noncomprehending parents no small amount of displeasure, the correspondence between him and Shaver continued for some time. A collection of those unpublished letters is and writings from Shaver are included in the aforementioned book, "The Reality of the Inner Earth," the cover of which shows a photo of Shaver superimposed over one of his mystically encoded rocks.

What did Shaver himself have to say about it all? In another new Global Communications release, called "The Smoky God and Other Inner Earth Mysteries," Shaver is quoted as saying of his reading public: "To me, struggling to find an opening out of the morass - no longer just for myself but now for all mankind - the flood of letters I received from other sufferers was a crushing blow, bringing hopeless despair. The caverns were not, I realized now, a localized thing. They extended underneath every area of the Earth. The evidence of their activity and strength piled up, until I could not help but conclude that there is no answer for present-day man. He cannot break their power over him, nor remedy the ills they visit upon him."

Shaver also writes in a similar pessimistic way about the UFOs, which first received worldwide attention with Kenneth Arnold's sighting in 1947, a few brief years after the publication of "I Remember Lemuria."

"The visits of the saucers," Shaver writes, "bring with them, for me, fresh despair. For I see them as proof of the caverns' contact with space. Knowing the cave people, I know that if any of the visiting saucers were benevolent visitors bringing gifts and knowledge to the surface people, they would be destroyed. To me, that explains the failure to contact our surface government, because those saucers that are not destroyed are our ancient enemies."

What Shaver is talking about is something similar to a concept first put forth by the late alien abduction researcher Budd Hopkins. Hopkins coined the phrase "confirmation anxiety" to describe what happens when an abductee finds proof of the reality of his experiences, such as seeing a mark left behind on his body after recalling that a skin sample had been taken during an abduction episode. A person needs to have some part of his mind in a state of doubt to function as a hiding place where he can call what he has experienced "unreal." When something happens to drive the troublesome memory into a place where the abductee cannot deny that something frightening and strange has really happened to him after all, when his "dreams" are confirmed for him, a whole new kind of anxiety kicks in.

Richard Shaver's death in November 1975 is also fraught with strange happenings. One of his followers and friends, a woman named Mary Jane Martin, knew him at the end. She said that his death was highly suspect, coming on the heels of his having just signed a contract to go to Hollywood and serve as a consultant on a movie about the deros and their Inner Earth kingdom of horror and shame. Shaver was very excited and had even bought new dentures for the occasion. Suddenly, he developed locked bowels and had to be hospitalized. He told his wife that the deros were trying to prevent his cinematic success and he would die there in the hospital. She assured him the operation was not a serious one and he would be fine.

Shaver's wife was quite correct and the surgery did go well. But as he lay recovering, Shaver suffered a pair of small heart attacks.

"Neither of which should have killed him," Martin said, "but he died in that hospital. His prediction came true. The deros would not let him live to make that movie."

But of course there remains an audience eager to know about the mysteries that so burdened Shaver. Timothy Beckley of Global Communications has made a sort of cottage industry out of interest in the Inner and Hollow Earth theories, saving some old and rare books from obscurity and publishing up-to-date compendiums written by more recent researchers.

And so it is left to us, decades after the deaths of Shaver and Palmer, to try to pick up the pieces and understand Shaver's torture in ways that can help us to deal with the very vocal evils of our own time. The ambitious reprinting efforts by Global Communications/Inner Light Books are an enormous help in those terms and well worth the effort involved in purchasing and reading the writings of a pioneer who seems at times to be whistling in the dark in a benighted, infernal hell, along with the rest of us.

SUGGESTED READING

RICHARD SHAVER: REALITY OF THE INNER EARTH

THE SMOKY GOD AND OTHER INNER EARTH MYSTERIES: EXPANDED EDITION

RICHARD SHAVER: CHILLING TALES FROM THE INNER EARTH

THE HIDDEN WORLD VOLUME 1: THE DERO! THE TERO! THE BATTLE BETWEEN GOOD AND EVIL UNDERGROUND

③

HAS THE MYSTERIOUS HOLE AT THE POLE BEEN PHOTOGRAPHED?
By Tim Cridland

The following chapter will be difficult to comprehend if the reader lacks familiarity with the Hollow Earth theory. The theory, in a nutshell, is that the Earth is hollow with large openings at the North and South Poles. The interior is lit by a small red "central sun" that keeps the climate at a constant tropical temperature. The inhabitants walk along the inner crust, held in place by the force of gravity. They are probably the pilots of flying saucers. The most widely available book on the subject is "The Hollow Earth," by Raymond Bernard. You are urged to read this book if you are unfamiliar with the subject.

HOLE-AT-THE-POLE PHOTOGRAPHS: AN OVERVIEW

The question most often asked by the uninitiated when discussing the Hollow Earth theory: "If there are holes at the poles, why aren't there any satellite photos of them?"

The usual response is to pull out the photos uncovered by Ray Palmer in the June 1970 issue of "Flying Saucers Magazine." Palmer, the man that some claim was responsible for starting the public's obsession with flying saucers, had started the modern-day Hollow Earth movement in an earlier issue of the magazine. Drawing on accounts of Admiral Byrd's polar flights as reported in the then-recently published "Worlds Beyond the Poles," by Amadeo F. Giannini, Palmer realized that Byrd's alleged reports of tropical conditions at the polar area fit in with conjectures about an inner world that were popular in the 19th century just as easily with Giannini's much more bizarre extended-space theory.

Palmer, upon finding the photo taken by the ESSA-7 satellite on November 23, 1968, declared "The North Pole photo, lacking clouds in the polar area, therefore reveals the surface of the planet. Although surrounding the polar area, and north of such areas as the North American continent and Greenland and the Asian continent, we can see the ice fields of the eight-foot thick ice . . . (in the photo) we do not see any ice fields in a large circular area directly at the geographic pole. Instead, we see-THE HOLE!"

There have been other satellite photos that are claimed to show a polar void, but not many from a polar orbit. Polar photos aren't very easy to find; there aren't many satellites in polar orbits, so this isn't that surprising. (Palmer claims that early troubles with polar-orbit satellites were due to miscalculations caused by the hole.) The polar photos that I've managed to find fall into four categories: 1. Jagged-edged un-photographed areas; 2. Fade to black night areas; 3. Complete cloud-cover; 4. Infrared and microwave. Palmer's "Flying Saucers" cover is an example of the first kind of photo. Although Palmer says that this is a photo of "the Hole," this is clearly not the case. It has been shown that this a composite photo-mosaic made from many satellite passes. This explains why the Earth is lit from all around. If this had been a single half, the globe would be dark; the half that is experiencing night. The dark area at the polar region has been explained as the 24-hour night that is experienced in the high northern latitudes in the winter months. I maintain that both of these interpretations are at odds with the facts.

This photo clearly does not show the Hole-at-the-Pole. According to Hollow Earth tradition, the interior of the Earth is illuminated by a small red "central sun." A photo taken directly above the pole, without cloud cover, should show the central sun shining brightly. This would seem to validate the polar-night explanation - if it weren't for some glaring inconsistencies. In Flora Benton's book, "Hollow Earth at the End Time," she points out that the ESSA-7 November 23rd photo could not have been taken on the claimed date "because it shows light reaching to approximately 76 degrees latitude. The North Cape of Norway, at 71 degrees, is in darkness for two months of every year, and these months would fall before and after December 22nd." A complete polar night photo would show a twilight area and a slow progression into the blackness of night, caused by the refraction of sunlight in the Earth's atmosphere.

This is evident in another photo that has been brought forth to boost the Hollow Earth position. This is clearly how a polar night should look. To understand Palmer's "Hole" photo we must look at another photo that to my knowledge has never been published before. This photos shows a jagged black area at the northern pole that, at one point, juts outward from a circular pattern. Clearly this is not a hole, unless a chunk of the polar rim has broken off and fallen into the Earth's interior. The dark area is also not polar night, unless there were some very extreme temperature inversions in the area of the jagged portion. It becomes obvious what is happening in these photos: the U.S. government is not photographing sections of the polar area. The question is raised: why? The implication: perhaps they don't want you to see the light from the central sun.

OUR HOLLOW EARTH

The next type of polar photo (type 3) that I've run across shows the polar area, fully lit but obscured by cloud cover. Palmer claims that the almost constant cloud cover is the reason that there are so few "Hole" shots. He even goes so far as to quote from the Bible to boost his position: Job 26:7,8. "He it was who spread the north above the void, and poised the Earth on nothingness. He fastens up the waters in his clouds, the mists do not tear apart under their weight."

This constant cloud cover can be easily understood from the Hollow Earth viewpoint; if the hollow interior of the Earth is temperate, as is claimed in Hollow Earth tradition, then the subzero air of the outer world meeting the almost tropical inner air would naturally form a dense mist.

When Palmer was writing, infrared satellite photography was nonexistent. Infrared photography would easily penetrate the clouds because it records heat, not light. Thus, if an infrared camera were to take a photo of the polar area from space, one would expect to see a hot area at the pole. Alas, this isn't what the first infrared polar shots show. What we do see is the aurora borealis surrounding the poles. Some of these photos show some unusual aurora formations, such as the time the aurora ring formed an O-shape with some bright concentrated areas.

Of course these photos don't rule out a Hollow Earth. Being government photos, if the government had photographed anything that they didn't want you to see, they would doctor the photos, as it appears happened with the earlier photos. Nonetheless, infrared photos haven't helped the Hollow Earth position either - that is, until now.

HOLE IN OZONE OVER SOUTH POLE WORRIES SCIENTISTS

A massive hole, initially reported by British scientists in March 1985, has been discovered in the ozone above the South Pole. This hole in the upper atmosphere, appearing each September and October, should be letting in hazardous cosmic rays in the south polar area. Atmospheric scientists are concerned that the hole may be growing in size, potentially threatening populated areas (shades of Alternative 3!)

"The Antarctic hole appears at the end of winter . . . by the end of November, the ozone, at altitudes of eight to sixteen miles, recovers. Each year, though, the hole has expanded, in 1985 reaching a size equivalent to the area of the United States." Infrared photos of the ozone hole look remarkably like what one would expect an infrared Hollow Earth photo to look like.

The cause of the hole is not yet understood. Theories of the cause of the ozone void range from volcanic particles and changes in solar activity to releases of chlorine and bromine gasses. "Some climate experts believe that a change in the motions of waves in cyclones in the upper atmosphere might cause the hole. For example, an upwelling of air over the pole could push aside the layer of the strato-

OUR HOLLOW EARTH

Photos, right and below, purporting to show the entrances to the inner world at the North and South Poles.

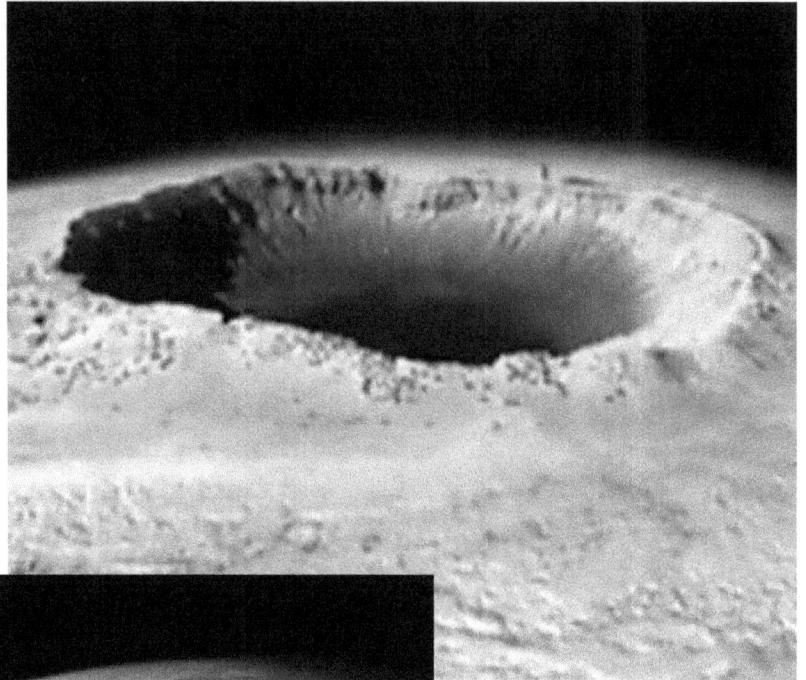

Several historical reports claim the Germans explored Antarctica before and during World War Two, and established huge bases under the ice.

sphere containing the most ozone, replacing it with low ozone air from lower altitudes . . . . Current climate models do not produce this effect."

"Off The Deep End" suggests that the cause of the hole in the atmosphere results directly from the hole-at-the-pole directly below it. The upwelling of air could come from directly underneath via the inner atmosphere. The upwelling is most probably caused by an interaction of the inner and outer atmospheres during the seasonal changes.

Another kind of polar photograph is the microwave photo. There exists an image of Antarctica produced by an ESMR (Electronically Scanning Microwave Radiometer) onboard the Nimbus 5 satellite. The ESMR device measures microwave radiation from the Earth's surface, using a meter-square scanner and a sensitive 1.55 cm wavelength receiver. As the scanner sweeps from side to side, an onboard computer halts it for a fraction of a second, takes measurement, and resumes the sweep. Each line of the image is made up of 78 such stops, completed every four seconds. At the wavelength used by ESMR, radiation penetrates the cloud cover and allows the surface brightness to be measured. The result is a map-like image recording neither heat nor light, but a quality known as "surface brightness temperature"- the relationship between the physical temperature of the target and the rate at which it gives off energy in the 1.55 cm band of the spectrum.

The brightness temperature variations from dark blue to magenta are not yet fully understood. Perhaps the reason that many scientists are confused by polar photos is because they do not allow for a Hollow Earth in their cosmos. Polar photos haven't hurt the Hollow Earth position at all, because each new photo demonstrates that the poles are, indeed, shrouded in mystery.

MORE HOLLOW EARTH INFO

Now and then people write to me and say "Stop printing all that Hollow Earth stuff. It's just ridiculous." Well, what's the use of calling my zine "Off The Deep End" if I can't print Hollow Earth stuff? Besides, I've got a torch to carry, as "The Hollow Hassle" hasn't published in years.

The February 22, 1993, issue of "TIME" has this to say about seismic studies of the shockwave produced by a recent nuclear blast: "Studies of the shockwave given off by the Chinese 0.66 megaton nuclear test have revealed a 'continent' 3,200 km underground." The article goes on to say that the word "continent" is used loosely. Apparently, they do not want us to confuse our inner and outer continents, but it then goes on to say: "What two scientists at the U.S. Geological Survey found was a region 320 km across and 130 km deep that is denser than the surrounding regions. The implication: the core-mantel boundary may be as complex as the Earth's surface."

OUR HOLLOW EARTH

In the National Oceanic and Atmospheric Administration publication entitled "Clouds" (NOAA/PA 71012), there is a most interesting set of photographs. Under the heading "The View From Above," there are three photographs of the Earth. One of the northern hemisphere, one of the southern hemisphere, and one of the equator. The implication of the text that accompanies these photos is that they can be combined to create an image of the whole Earth.

The problem is that the images of both Poles show a black space where cloud cover should be. According to debunkers, this blackness is simply how a satellite mosaic shows the 24-hour night at the Poles. The problem with this is that there can never be night at both Poles at the same time. Yet this is what seems to be claimed in the text. Something is wrong here.

A man for all reasons: The enigmatic Tim Cridland.

Follow the author on Facebook:

www.facebook.com/ZamoraTKing

TIM R. SWARTZ:
THE HOLLOW EARTH TOURIST
By Sean Casteel

Tim Swartz's interest in UFOs began in his childhood, but not in the way you might expect. Way back in 1968, his third grade class was told to give reports on current events, and Swartz was assigned an article on a UFO flap that was ongoing at the time.

"I didn't know anything about UFOs," he recalled, "and didn't really care about UFOs. But I gave my report and was just instantly pegged for the rest of my life by my fellow students as 'the Flying Saucer Guy.' I was the guy who believed in little green men and Martians. Even though I didn't know a flying saucer from Adam. But that was the role I was given."

But the interesting part was still to come. Some of the same people who laughed at Swartz when others were around would later approach him and quietly talk about their own UFO and ghost experiences. It became a familiar pattern for Swartz.

"They wanted somebody to listen to their story," he said, "and basically just tell them they're not crazy. Then they go off and you can tell that a huge weight has been lifted."

The fact that so many people were telling surprisingly similar stories brought it home to Swartz that something must really be going on. He would end up, of course, dedicating a large portion of his life to the subject.

I knew going in that Swartz has a history of traveling the world seeking the answers to various paranormal mysteries. When I asked him about exactly where he had gone, he laughed and said "I've been everywhere, man."

It all began in the 1980s, when Swartz worked as a videographer and producer for a PBS station in Indianapolis, Indiana, their local Channel 20, which was

the flagship station at the time for all the other PBS stations in the state. The station had a for-profit arm that would hire out their film crews to other production companies, which led to Swartz working for all the major networks in the U.S. and even some foreign networks. Swartz also worked as an official videographer for the State of Indiana, specifically for then-governor Evan Bayh.

While working for a Channel 20 syndicated program called "The Morning Ag Report," Swartz was tapped to be part of the overseas film crew that accompanied state and federal agriculture officials on fact-finding trips far and wide. The list of countries Swartz visited is long, and includes England, Germany, Poland, Bulgaria, Turkey, Russia, Hong Kong, China, Japan, South Korea, Egypt and Nairobi.

In preparation for many of those overseas assignments, Swartz would set up meetings with local researchers and experts involved with UFOs and other types of paranormal investigation.

"For example, in Egypt," Swartz said, "I met with somebody from Cairo who was familiar with a lot of tunnels and other things that government officials don't talk about. And they don't like it being broadcast to the tourists that these things are there. We got to examine some of these unique places on the Giza Plateau that not everybody gets a chance to see."

In the early 1990s, Swartz made the acquaintance of another Tim, Timothy Green Beckley, and began to write articles for Beckley's "UFO Universe Magazine" as well as writing numerous books for Beckley's publishing house, Global Communications. Swartz also wrote screenplays and did some directing and videography work for Beckley's line of horror movies, with titles like "The Curse of Ed Wood" and "Skin-Eating Jungle Vampires."

The theory of the Hollow Earth was also of great interest to Swartz, and, beginning as a youth, he read voraciously on the subject - like Tarzan creator Edgar Rice Burroughs' "Pellucidar" series of action/adventure books set in a fictional Hollow Earth where prehistoric animals and various tribes of humans dwelt.

"Burroughs obviously did his research," Swartz said. "Because he had the polar openings and how the inner Earth is bathed in perpetual sunlight because the sun that hung in the sky there could never set. It always looked like you were living in the bottom of a giant bowl. There was a telepathic master race that kept everyone else enslaved. Just wonderful adventure books for teenagers."

Meanwhile, in the nonfiction world, Beckley had written "The Shaver Mystery and the Inner Earth" for legendary paranormal publisher Gray Barker, and it was a must-read for Swartz.

The Hollow Earth theory continued to transform and evolve, and Swartz and Beckley's writing kept pace with the changes.

"By the 1990s, you had all kinds of interesting things," Swartz said, "like the idea of secret military underground bases and the possibility that there are aliens underground controlling things. It's amazing how something that originated in the 19th century is still with us today. It's just taken on different personas and become intertwined with the whole UFO mystery."

Swartz has become the "resident expert" for Global Communications on Admiral Byrd and the Hollow Earth mystery, having penned such page-turners as "The Secret Lost Diary of Admiral Richard E. Byrd and the Phantom of the Poles" and "Admiral Byrd's Secret Journey Beyond the Poles." What follows is Swartz fielding questions about a subject that has long fascinated him and which likely has come to fascinate you as well.

*   *   *   *

Question: Can you give me some biographical background on Admiral Byrd? What kind of career did he have prior to his going to the South Pole? Why was it deemed appropriate for him to lead the expedition?

Swartz: Well, before he was Admiral Byrd, he was Richard Evelyn Byrd, Jr. and he was born in 1888. He was born right in that time when the Wright Brothers were doing their innovative work with airplanes. Byrd was extremely fascinated by airplanes and he learned to fly fairly early on. He recognized the potential of airplanes - not only for commercial reasons but for military reasons as well. So Byrd was one of the early forerunners to promote the idea of using airplanes for military purposes.

Byrd graduated from the Naval Academy in 1912 and was commissioned an ensign in the U.S. Navy. His first assignment was on the battleship the U.S.S. Wyoming. By the time World War I rolled around, he was technically retired, but Byrd was able to serve as a retired officer on active duty. He volunteered to become a naval aviator. He took flying lessons and earned his pilot's wings in 1917. This was something he had wanted to do for a long, long time.

Byrd had also been interested in exploration. By that time, most of the world had already been pretty much explored. He had been an avid reader since he was young of adventure books, books detailing expeditions to, say, Africa, South America, overseas expeditions. He'd always been fascinated with that. By his time, the only things that were left to explore would be the Polar Regions. Since the early 19th century, there had been explorations of the North and South Pole to try to discover what was there. But Byrd figured that, with his expertise, especially with aircraft, that he would be able to make inroads into further exploration of the Polar Regions.

His first trip was in 1926, when, along with a pilot named Floyd Bennett, he attempted to fly over the North Pole in a tri-motor monoplane. He had been financed by the Ford Motor Company to make this flight. It lasted about fourteen to fifteen hours, and they claimed to have reached the North Pole, covering a distance of about 1,500 miles. The encircled it and then managed to make it back safely. So when he returned to the U.S., he was a national hero. You know, in 1926, this was the Roaring Twenties, when people were eager for new and different things. So the U.S. embraced Byrd as a national hero. Congress even passed a special act that promoted him to the rank of commander, and then they awarded him the National Medal of Honor. From that point on, to the U.S., Byrd could do no wrong, even though, years later, there has been doubt cast on whether or not they actually made this flight over the North Pole as they said they had. It's one of those things that haters are going to hate, I suppose. There's no way to know, other than their word, whether they actually made it as close to the North Pole as possible. I'm going to give them the benefit of the doubt. Naturally, it's easy to criticize somebody after they're dead and gone and they can't defend themselves.

In 1927, Byrd announced he was going to make a transatlantic flight with the backing of private investors. So again, with pilot Floyd Bennett and some other crew members, he was attempting a transatlantic flight. But unfortunately, during one of the test runs, Byrd' airplane crashed and it was Charles Lindberg who actually ended up reaching that particular milestone first in 1927. Then later on, Byrd actually did complete a flight across the Atlantic from June 29 to July 1 in 1927. He was again given great honor in the U.S. when he returned and was awarded the Distinguished Flying Cross by the then-Secretary of the Navy. After that, Byrd's interest turned towards Antarctica. He was involved in the first Antarctic expedition in 1930. This involved two ships and three airplanes. The idea was for it to be a photographic and geological expedition to try to establish whether there was anything in Antarctica mineral-wise that might be useful. Byrd was involved in at least three Antarctic expeditions before Operation High Jump, so he was no stranger to Antarctica. In fact, on his second Antarctic expedition, in 1934, he spent five winter months alone operating a meteorological station. He almost died from carbon monoxide poisoning because the stove he had malfunctioned.

Question: This was around the time when Byrd visited Nazi Germany?

Swartz: Yes, in late 1938, Byrd actually visited Nazi Germany because he was invited to participate in the 1938-1939 German Antarctic expedition. And he was wined and dined. The Germans had been very impressed by Byrd's knowledge and experience regarding Antarctica. But due to the political conditions at the time, Byrd declined. But then the Germans continued not only with that expedition but also a number of others, probably establishing several bases in the region, beginning then and lasting through the duration of World War II.

THE MYSTERIES SURROUNDING OPERATION HIGH JUMP

Question: So now tell me about Operation High Jump.

Swartz: Operation High Jump was first conceived in 1946, shortly after the end of World War II. Secretary of the Navy James Forestall appointed Byrd his officer-in-charge of Antarctic development. Operation High Jump is extremely odd over-all. Considering that, at the time, right after the end of World War II, the Navy was decommissioning a lot of ships, putting lots of them in mothballs. There really wasn't any reason to use them anymore. And then suddenly Secretary Forestall said we need to get a lot of these ships back into operation again because we're going to make this "scientific" expedition to Antarctica.

To date, it's been the largest such expedition ever. It was expected to last six to eight months, which is a huge amount of time. This expedition was supported by a huge naval force and commanded by Rear Admiral Richard Cruzen. There were thirteen U.S. Navy support ships, six helicopters, six flying boats, two seaplanes and fifteen other aircraft. Plus probably 4,000 personnel going along for this so-called "scientific" expedition. You have to understand, this was an enormous operation. And that's where the mystery begins. Why would you need such a gargantuan naval force for just an exploratory scientific expedition?

And, of course, anyone can speculate about this in many different ways and they have. But the expedition arrived in December 1946. They made explorations using airplanes of an area about the size of the U.S. They discovered ten new mountain ranges and gathered an amazing amount of information. One really unusual thing about all this is that they arrived in December 1946 and, in about three weeks' time, they decided they were done exploring, even though they were originally supposed to be there around six months.

No real official explanation has ever been given about why they suddenly decided to leave that quickly. In that short time, they did accomplish a lot of things, and if they had stayed longer, what more might they have discovered? Some people have speculated that they went there in search of a secret Nazi base hidden somewhere along the coast of Antarctica. At the end of World War II, there were a number of German U-boats that had left the Canary Islands carrying personnel, equipment, supplies and things like that. They would later surrender in Argentina but without all this personnel and equipment onboard. Now, one of the U-boat captains said that they had dropped off their people, equipment, etc. at a secret base in Antarctica. And declassified documents show that this could be one of the reasons why this expedition Operation High Jump had been established, to find out just what was going on in Antarctica.

SUSPECTED NAZI INVOLVEMENT

You have to realize that at the time, just after the end of World War II, there were Nazi officials, intelligence officers, scientists, high-ranking officers who had disappeared out of Europe. And speculation had it that they were heading to South America. A lot of them didn't show up in South America, so the U.S. and the Allied Forces wanted to know where they were. One of the big fears was that they had established something like a Fourth Reich command somewhere in Antarctica. So there's a possibility that Operation High Jump had been basically a military operation to ascertain whether this was true or not. And if it was true, then the response was to invade, take it over, or perhaps even conduct a diplomatic mission. Because if this was true, if a lot of high-ranking scientists and Nazi officials had escaped to Antarctica, this would have been gold to get ahold of, especially by the U.S. These were people that would have been highly prized for various reasons. So we have to get these people and get them alive. And we also have to get the possible equipment and secret weaponry that may have been taken out of Europe and hidden away in Antarctica.

So there's a very good possibility with Operation High Jump that this was the real reason that they were there. The speculation over the years has been that one of the reasons they left early was that Operation High Jump had been ambushed by, say, Nazi flying saucers or some kind of secret weaponry and they were driven away. I have not uncovered any decent evidence to show that's true. This expedition had over 4,000 men, and something like that would be very difficult to keep secret. Even though, with the sailors, it's part of their job to agree not to talk. But, as you've seen, especially with the UFO mystery, you have a lot of people who may have been involved in UFO recovery that on their deathbed admitted that, "Yeah, yeah, this was actually true."

But these men associated with Operation High Jump did not mention anything about being attacked or other members of their crew being killed by some kind of Nazi attack or whatever. So there's a good possibility that they went there and didn't find what they were looking for. Or they DID find what they were looking for, but it wasn't as big of an operation or secret base as they thought it was going to be. Based on the testimony of the German U-boat captain, this was a pretty good-sized base and was being manned by several thousand high-ranking and elite German squadrons. And it was heavily fortified and heavily protected.

You have to understand that Antarctica is not a pleasant place to live, and it's extremely difficult to establish any kind of large operation there. You have to consider the huge amount of fuel that has to be used just to keep warm every day. So unless the Germans had actually discovered an underground cavern system, which is one of the possibilities that has been talked about over the years, and that this cavern system was warmed by, say, volcanic springs, something along those lines, then more than likely this so-called secret base in Antarctica wasn't actually there and the secret Nazi operation at the end of World War II had actually established itself in South America. The whole Antarctica thing may have just been a red herring situation.

Nazi Germany had been interested in Antarctica during World War II because of the possibility that there was some kind of entranceway into the Hollow Earth there. Hitler had sent a number of expeditions around the world, especially to places like Tibet and Nepal and parts of South America, in search of these entranceways into the Hollow Earth because their occult beliefs had it that the Hollow Earth was populated by the Root Race, the Aryan people. Hitler and his cronies believed that the Aryans were the rightful owners of the world and that they originated from some kind of Super Race that lived in some kind of underground super-civilization. And that there were entranceways, especially around the Himalayas, South America and possibly even Antarctica. So a number of expeditions had been sent to these areas to try to find these entranceways, to get down in there and establish contact with their ancestors, basically, is what they believed. And then hopefully to establish diplomatic relations and to get help in winning the war against the rest of us slovenly bunch.

Let me backtrack a little. The story since the 19th century was that there are openings at the North and South Polar Regions and that these openings are large enough that you could walk or fly into them without even realizing that you had done so. Now here in the 21st century, unless there has been really a massive disinformation campaign going on and photographs of the area have been doctored - I'm not saying that that's not possible, but I'm saying that's unlikely - it's probably not true that these mythical polar openings actually exist. Especially in the Arctic regions because it's all ocean there. It would be a little more difficult, I suppose, to have a giant opening into the Hollow Earth.

At Antarctica, on the other hand, there could actually BE an opening into a cavernous world. You have mountains and it's a giant landmass down there. There have been satellite photographs taken that show some kind of opening in Antarctica and some kind of southern polar light is coming out of this giant cavern. It could very well be that one of these Nazi expeditions actually did discover one of these cavern entranceways into a subterranean part of the world. Whether or not they really made contact with underground dwellers - that remains to be seen.

GREEN AND PLEASANT AND VERY STRANGE

Question: What about Admiral Byrd stumbling into a green and pleasant land? Was that his eventual discovery of the Hollow Earth? When did all that "high strangeness" kick in?

Swartz: That "high strangeness" kicked in with his book "The Secret Lost Diaries of Admiral Byrd," which alleged that in 1947 he was conducting a flight over the northern polar areas. Actually, he was at the South Pole with Operation High Jump. There's this kind of curious discrepancy here.

Question: So he was at the North Pole in secret? The world didn't know he was there?

Swartz: Possibly. My speculation is that this alleged "secret diary" was actually released in a disinformation campaign to draw attention away from what was happening with Operation High Jump. Because whatever happened in Antarctica with Operation High Jump, it was decided that the information was important and had to be kept secret. Especially in the late 1950s and on into the 1960s, when a lot of information about Operation High Jump was starting to leak out a little bit, I think this book, "Secret Lost Diaries," had been written in an attempt to discredit the whole scenario.

We've seen that, again, with the UFO phenomenon, where the military, the government, intelligence officials - who knows? - have released information that is a little bit true and a lot false. The false part is so wild and crazy that it then tends to discredit everything. And that may be what is going on with this, that this whole story about Byrd flying over the North Pole and seeing areas of forest and prehistoric creatures and warm, almost tropical areas, having flown into the Hollow Earth - this may actually have been part of a campaign to discredit the stories that were starting to leak out concerning Operation High Jump. If you have these obviously wild stories of Byrd flying into the Hollow Earth and then juxtapose them with Operation High Jump, then people are going to disbelieve them both.

So if the stories come out that the Operation High Jump expedition found some kind of Nazi enclave in Antarctica and then had to come back to the U.S. extremely quickly, that's information that you don't want to leak out. So you go and combine that, then, with the Hollow Earth story where Byrd's plane was basically shanghaied by flying discs with swastikas on them, taken into the Hollow Earth and then given a meeting with the Hollow Earth people and being told basically the same kinds of stories that the UFO contactees were being told. That they were afraid of our atomic experiments and that if we persisted with them we were going to destroy ourselves. Then they possibly may have to come out from their secret cities underground and take over to stop us from doing that.

BYRD'S WARNING AND THE DAWN OF THE MODERN UFO ERA

I don't know. I really do think that the whole Hollow Earth part of this story is manufactured, that it did not happen like the popular stories have it. Instead it's being used to cover up whatever it was that happened to Byrd and his expedition Operation High Jump in Antarctica. Because when Byrd came back to the U.S., he was extremely concerned. He warned that the U.S. should adopt measures to protect us from the possibility of an invasion by hostile planes and missiles coming from the Polar Regions. He said he wasn't trying to scare us, but the cruel reality was that, in the case of a new war, the U.S. could be attacked by enemies flying over one or both poles. He gave a talk to Congress, and this was a secret talk. It was recorded that he gave this talk, but no transcripts have ever been released of just exactly what Byrd told the House and Senate during this official enquiry into what had happened in Antarctica. I don't think it's a coincidence as well that later that year, in July 1947, some kind of unusual aircraft crashed at Roswell.

A lot of present day writers will say that Byrd was afraid that Russia or China would send missiles or fly planes over the poles to attack the U.S. He didn't say that. He just warned against "enemies" attacking us FROM - he didn't say FLYING OVER - he said FROM the North or South Pole. Something happened that spooked him, but what that is, who knows? That's the whole conundrum about all of this. They weren't spooked like they'd been attacked and ships sank and planes crashed and personnel were killed. That didn't happen. But they were spooked enough that they left really early and then came back and warned the U.S. about some kind of invasion coming from the Polar Regions. And then, just a few months later, the whole modern UFO era started. And then you have the crash at Roswell of whatever that was. In the early days of the UFO mystery, especially with the crash at Roswell, the idea of this being extraterrestrial aircraft was not talked about. Instead there was the fear that these were Nazi aircraft or Nazi aircraft that had been found and were now being flown by the Soviet Union. It wasn't until later the whole extraterrestrial hypothesis started to come out.

So I think that a lot of these stories that deal with Byrd allegedly discovering an entranceway into the Hollow Earth are cover stories to deflect what was really going on. And I can only speculate about what was really going on, but I think it does have something to do with the Nazis and Nazi secret weapons. Whether or not they did discover a secret base in Antarctica, or maybe a small one - because I think the main operations were taking place out of South America. Especially in Argentina, where the Peron government was extremely friendly to the Nazis. A lot of Nazis escaped to Argentina at the end of the war, including lots of Nazi scientists who were in Argentina actually working to reestablish a Fourth Reich. We do know that they were trying to develop atomic weapons and they were also continuing their flying disc operations. It could very well be that the whole Antarctic thing was a misdirection.

One other thing that I should add to all this is that in 1968, even though there was an international provision not to conduct atomic tests in Antarctica, the U.S. exploded at least one and possibly several nuclear weapons in Antarctica in the areas where it had been alleged that these Nazi bases were located. And, again, that's one of these things where they weren't supposed to do that, the information was kind of occluded, but they did. It's rife for speculation. But why would the U.S. explode an atomic weapon in Antarctica when international treaties forbid it?

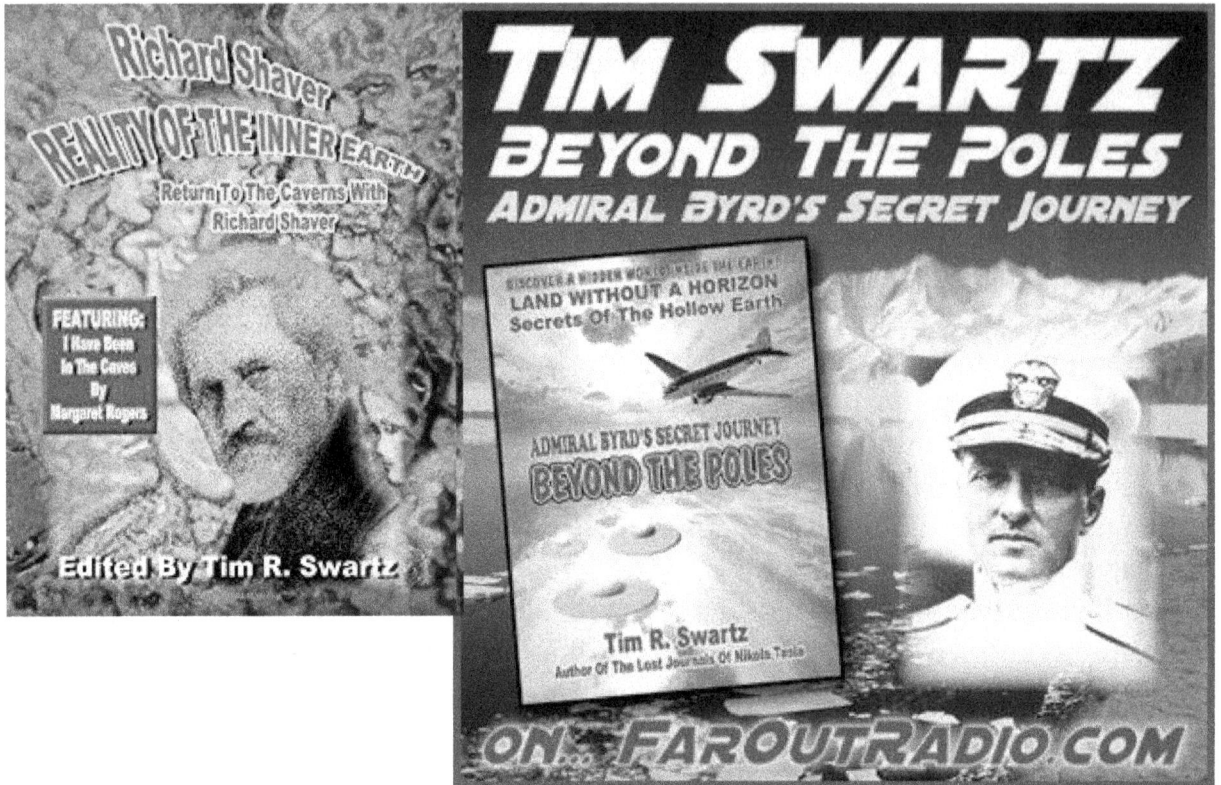

Tim Swartz has written numerous books on hollow/inner earth topics.
The Shaver Mystery has been one of his favorite subjects.

Swartz is an award winning producer.

Tim at Great Pyramid.

On the air as co-host of Exploring the Bizarre (KCORradio.com).

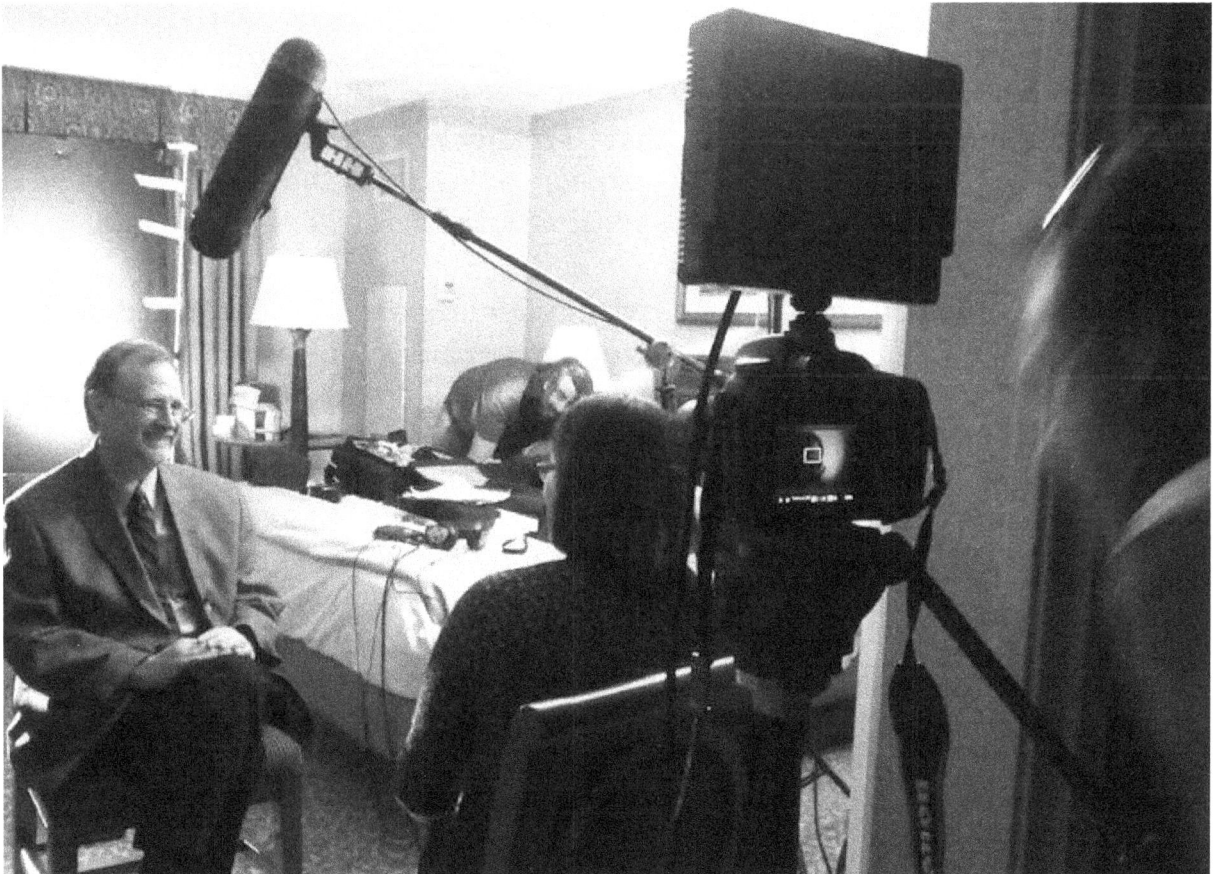

OUR HOLLOW EARTH

DID THE NAZIS STEAL TECHNOLOGY FROM NIKOLA TESLA?

Question: Recently you and publisher/author Tim Beckley produced a book "Nazi UFO Time Travelers." In this very intriguing title you bring up the idea that the Germans who came over under Operation Paperclip might have created a secret space program that might have been responsible for several UFO crashes - including the one outside of Roswell. How did you go about developing this theory and are some of the UFOs seen in our sky the results of Nazi handiwork?

Swartz: Operation Paperclip was the secret U.S. program in which more than 1,600 German scientists, engineers, and intelligent officers were recruited and brought to the United States for government employment from post-Nazi Germany. The primary purpose for Operation Paperclip was for the U.S. to gain a military and science advantage over the Soviet Union. Even though President Truman issued orders that no Germans who were Nazis during the war be allowed into, or to work for, the U.S., Operation Paperclip overruled that order and turned a blind eye to the fact that most who were brought to the U.S. had been (and probably still were) Nazis.

German scientists had made some amazing leaps in scientific knowledge during WWII, including the development of highly advanced aircraft and possibly even ships that could travel outside of Earth's atmosphere. The Nazis had a spy ring established on the East coast of the U.S. just before and during the war. One branch of this clandestine organization was dedicated to finding and stealing new and developing technology that could prove useful in their wartime effort. One notable prize that they were able to make off with was a sizable cache of notes and papers from Nikola Tesla. It appears that Germany was able to develop field propulsion technology from Tesla's early experiments and use this to develop a new form of aircraft that may have been responsible for some of the early UFO sightings around the world.

There were reports from Allied servicemen who were tasked with finding and identifying secret Nazi technology. Among this material that had been shipped back to the U.S. were strange disc-shaped aircraft that looked nothing like conventional planes or V-2 rockets. Apparently, some of the German scientists who had been brought to the U.S. had heard about these flying discs, but none had worked on their development. When UFOs began to be sighted starting in 1947, it was assumed that these were being flown by remnants of the Third Reich who had managed to escape to secret locations in Antarctica and South America. After these "UFOs" had been recovered by the U.S. military, there was a radical jump in scientific understanding on what we now call anti-gravity. Unfortunately, this scientific development has been kept secret from the civilian sector and more-than-likely has been used exclusively by the military.

After the crash at Roswell (and several other locations), the rumor began to circulate that UFOs were extraterrestrial spaceships. However, this may have been a disinformation campaign to hide the fact that UFOs were manmade, secret technology aircraft being operated by Germans who were attempting to establish the Fourth Reich. Of course, Walter Bosley has done some excellent research on the idea that the development of secret, non-conventional aircraft can be traced as far back as the middle of the 19th century by a Bavarian group run almost like a secret society. This group may be one of two "breakaway civilizations" that have been operating on the fringes of our society for years.

GERMAN-SPEAKING ARYAN ALIENS

Question: Isn't it true that some of the early contactees claim the "space people" they met spoke with a German accent? Didn't the boot print of the man from Venus George Adamski claims to have met have the imprint of a swastika on the bottom of the sole? Were some of these contactees unknowingly having encounters with Nazi engineers?

Swartz: One of the curious things about the early contactees were their descriptions of the "Space Brothers," which almost invariably were tall, fair-skinned, blue-eyed and blond. This was the epitome of the Nazi belief of the perfect Aryan person. One of the first contactees, George Adamski, achieved national fame when he began to have visits from the Space Brothers who wanted him to be their spokesman. They told him they were from Venus and stressed the importance of stopping all nuclear testing and living in peace and harmony. Once, Adamski overheard the Space Brothers speaking to each other in fluent German. Being from Poland, he spoke some German, and easily recognized it as such. When he questioned the Brothers they answered that they spoke all the languages of Earth. Adamski and other contactees also said that alien writing they saw onboard the flying saucers looked remarkably like the old Nordic alphabet...including the swastika.

Then you had the Nebraskan Farm-Broker, Reinhold Schmidt, who on November 5, 1957, encountered a UFO that caused his car to break down out in the middle of nowhere. The landed UFO, which Schmidt described as looking like a "half-filled balloon," shot out a beam of light that struck him in the middle of his chest, causing instant paralysis. Schmidt was taken inside the craft where there were six occupants who spoke English with a German accent.

Schmidt would later write that when the occupants spoke among themselves they used High German, which he happened to understand. What is interesting is that Schmidt did not consider his experience as a contact with extraterrestrials; he thought that the ship was Russian, manned by a group of German scientists. After going to the authorities about his experience, a press release was issued stating that a "spaceship" had landed near Kearney, Nebraska. This surprised

Schmidt since he had said nothing about seeing a spaceship. Afterwards, after being interviewed by two Air Force officers, Schmidt was taken in front of a mental competency board and committed to a psychiatric hospital. Apparently, the Air Force was not happy that Schmidt reported seeing Germans in a UFO and not spacemen from the planet Venus.

Question: How did the Nazis go about developing time travel, if they have it? I understand they had a team of female mediums who were channeling Aryan space beings as early as 1919.

Swartz: The idea that Germany may have achieved anti-gravity technology before and during WWII seems pretty amazing. But the idea that they may have also been able to take the first steps towards workable time travel is almost unbelievable. Before Hitler came to power, National Socialists had been developing projects meant to find the origins of the Aryans and the location of legendary Shamballa. They expected to obtain some secret knowledge to seize domination over the world. Secret expeditions were sent to Tibet and the Himalayas, and the number of such expeditions increased when the Nazis came to power in 1933.

The secret projects were especially active in the years 1935-1939, and probably continued even after the war campaign in Europe started. But all the documents pertaining to the projects were destroyed before Nazi Germany capitulated or possibly are still being kept hidden in undisclosed places.

FEMALE PSYCHICS CHANNELING FOR A NAZI FUTURE

It has been suggested that some Nazi expedition came across a wrecked UFO and contacted its crew somewhere along the line. Others speculate that contacts between Germans and extraterrestrials happened much earlier. In the early 1900s, "The All German Society for Metaphysics" (Alldeutsche Gesellschaft fr Metaphysik) were a group of woman spirit mediums who were involved in extraterrestrial telepathic contact. The society was later renamed the "Vril Society" or "Society of Vrilerinnen Women." The head of this group was Maria Orsitsch, who claimed that in 1917 she made contact with extraterrestrials from a distant solar system called Aldebaran.

Maria said that she received, via medium transmissions, technical data for the construction of a circular flight machine. In late November 1924, Maria Orsitsch visited Rudolf Hess in his apartment in Munich and revealed that they were already in the process of building a spacecraft based on this channeled information. Because of the sanctions placed on Germany after WWI, parts to build their spacecraft were slow to come in. This difficulty continued with the rise of Hitler and the Nazi Party, who placed a ban on secret societies in 1941.

In December 1943 Maria attended a secret meeting at the seaside resort of Kolberg. The main purpose of the meeting was to deal with the Aldebaran project.

OUR HOLLOW EARTH

The Vril mediums had received precise information regarding the habitable planets around the Aldebaran sun and they were willing to plan a trip there. By 1944, high-ranking Nazi officials had been brought into the fold, and in January, there was a meeting between Hitler, Himmler, and Dr. W. Schumann (scientist and professor in the Technical University of Munich) where it was decided that a Vril 7 Jaeger spaceship would attempt a flight to Aldebaran.

The Vril 7 Jaeger spaceship was allegedly able to circumnavigate the speed of light by warping time-space. Essentially, it was a time machine. A test flight in late 1944 apparently almost ended in disaster as the ship returned damaged and "looking as if it had been flying for hundreds of years."

Not much is known after this point. Maria Orsitsch disappeared and there are only rumors about what happened to the Vril 7 Jaeger spaceship. The Nazi "Bell" may have been an independent development by the German military to weaponize time travel using the Vril Societies channeled information.

No one can say for sure if the Nazis actually had contacts with aliens or not. Defense technology and economy experts state that, at the end of the 1930s, Germany possessed just 57 submarines, and over the four years of WWII it built 1,163 modern, technologically-advanced submarines at its dockyards and even put them into operation. How was that possible when Germans were short of materials for waging war, and under the condition of terrible bombing by Allied forces? One may also wonder why Nazis did not create more perfect technologies with the assistance of extraterrestrial intellect. In fact, the Germans used only technologies that required a short production period.

Nazis created the first jet-propelled aircraft that could make up to 1,000 km/h and was superior to any airplane known in the anti-Hitler coalition. It is a mystery how Germans managed to produce 2,000 new fighting machines over the few months of 1945.

As for manmade flying saucers, the U.S. war archives and the British Air Force archives contain a great number of reports from military pilots who said they came across strange flying apparatuses resembling British military helmets when flying over Germany. American Kenneth Arnold, who is known as the UFO "discoverer," was not the first contemporary who witnessed flying saucers in the sky. British and American pilots witnessed the phenomenon during WWII. Firing at such objects did not damage them at all!

On October 14, 1943, British Air Force Major R. Holmes reported that he witnessed several "big bright discs" during bombardment of Schweinfurt. And the objects did not respond to firing. Pilots of U.S. Air Force interceptors who flew over the German territory in the winter of 1945 also witnessed UFOs. These days, some authors insist that the above episodes prove that the Third Reich had secret weapons at its disposal. They also refer to German designers Schriever, Habermol,

OUR HOLLOW EARTH

Miethe and Belluzzo, who were said to be working on flying discs since 1941. But reputable aviation experts denied this version. They said that even modern technologies did not allow production of aircraft as invulnerable and speedy as those objects. Indeed, the experts were absolutely right, but they did not consider the fact that Germans could have created the apparatuses after a contact with aliens.

WAS A NAZI THE WORLD'S FIRST ASTRONAUT?

Raul Streicher, 85, from Germany made a sensational statement in Der Spiegel in 2000. The old man insisted that it was he who was in fact the number one spaceman, not Soviet Yuri Gagarin! He added that he had been first in orbit in 1945. That sounded like an absolute fable, and Der Spiegel launched a special investigation of the case and studied classified archives of the Third Reich. The investigation proved that the old man was not lying.

Before WWII, Germany set up a network of secret research institutes to develop and improve arms and methods of impact on humans. In 1938, a specialized rocket engineering research institute was founded near Wewelsburgh where the SS headquarters were located. Reich's Marshal Gering was the curator of the institute that designed the panzerfaust, the Panzerknakke pocket grenade cup discharge and various war missiles, including the Fau-3 missile complex. Nazis pinned great hopes in the latter, as the A9/A10 cruise missile that was part of the complex could be used either as intercontinental (Hitler planned to destroy New York in the summer of 1945) or as a space rocket.

Test launching of the missile took place in 1943, but the invention turned out to be technically imperfect and sixteen out of the eighteen launched missiles exploded at take-off or in the air. Next year, the research institute produced about 40 improved missiles. At the same time, the Fuehrer ordered the recruitment of military astronauts among German aces. A new squadron consisting of from 100 to 500 pilots was formed in March 1944. Raul Streicher was also among them.

After several successful tests of the rockets in 1944, the final selection of astronauts was made. Hitler chose two candidates by referring to their personal horoscopes, as he was fond of astrology. Those were Martin von Dulen and Raul Streicher, and the Fuehrer obviously sympathized with the latter. A rocket with von Dulen onboard was first launched on February 18, 1945. The rocket exploded about three minutes after takeoff. In six days another rocket with Raul Streicher onboard was successfully launched, orbited the Earth and landed on water in Japan. So, Streicher says that his flight on February 24, 1945, was the beginning of space exploration by humans.

When the Nazis realized that their war campaign was lost they decided to blow up a small cosmo-drome near Wewelsburg and planned to shelter the results of their investigations and some of the scientists with the secret research institute in a castle in the Carpathian Mountains. The leader of the research institute was the owner of the castle and he hoped to continue researches there after the end of the war and some day gain revenge. But the sweeping advance of the Allied forces frustrated the plans. American forces seized the head of the research institute, and Soviet troops got some of the rockets designed by the institute. Later they were used in development of the Soviet space program.

There was an order to liquidate Streicher as he knew too much. The astronaut was in hiding in Eastern Europe for some time and then after several years settled in GDR. After Yuri Gagarin's first flight into space in 1961, Streicher announced that it was he and not the Soviet astronaut who must be considered the pioneer of space. However, the man failed to provide any evidence to prove that he was telling the truth.

Question: Did the Nazis ever get to the moon?

Swartz: After World War II, rumors circulated that German astronauts had traveled to the moon and established a top-secret facility there. There were several different aeronautical programs going on in Germany during WWII that involved disc-shaped craft. One was the Vril project I mentioned earlier that used a unique propulsion system to warp time and space. The other German projects researched conventional jet/rocket propulsion and field propulsion.

Question: I know Tim Beckley has posted his thought that some of the early UFO groups may have been trying to cover up a Nazi/UFO connection by pushing the theory that the flying saucers, if they existed, were from far off worlds. Do you think Major Keyhoe and the NICAP staff knew what was really going on and tried to divert attention from a more earthbound theory?

Swartz: I don't know. I think that the disinformation campaign about UFOs has been so successful over the years that we may never know the truth. There did seem to be an effort almost from the beginning to lead investigators away from any other possibility other than UFOs are extraterrestrial. That, or they are hoaxes and misidentifications of known objects. Any other explanation, like the idea that they are human-constructed, top secret aircraft/spacecraft, was always quickly discounted. This despite the fact that Army Air Force and Navy officers worried early on that UFOs were some sort of high technology of the Nazis or from the Soviet Union using captured Nazi equipment.

Question: After all is said and done, is the Earth hollow in your opinion? Ringed by a vast system of tunnels and chambers?

Swartz: I wish I could give a definitive answer to that question. I don't think the Earth is completely hollow, like it was imagined by Edgar Rice Burroughs in his Pellucidar series of books where the Earth is a hollow shell with the inner world as the internal surface of that shell. However, I have never been there, so I can't say for sure. I do believe that there are vast series of tunnels and large chambers throughout the planet, and that many seem to be thousands, if not millions, of years old. There have been hundreds of people throughout history that have visited these amazing structures and have made it back to tell about them. So I am inclined to believe that this is a fact.

OUR HOLLOW EARTH

5

**RIVERS OF THE UNDERWORLD -
A HALO PARANORMAL
INVESTIGATION**

THE RIVER WILL GUIDE YOU HOME
By Deanna Jaxine Stinson

POEM:

Waters flow in structured lines
Boats rushing through pools of time
Into caves of twilight breathe
Carved out by hands of destiny
Rushing over my memories
Blood through veins
Palm tree keys
Deliver me to
This epiphany

THE RIVERS OF THE UNDERWORLD

In Greek Mythology, it is told that five rivers exist which go into the underworld. These rivers are as follows; Acheron, Cocytus, Lethe, Phlegethon, and Styx. These rivers are a part of Hades; who also is King there. The rivers guide us to where we are meant to be in the afterlife. Just like in life, we are born from a watery womb, guided by the blood flowing through our veins into birth.

The following list will help you to better understand.

Acheron- This River is also understood as a watery body of woe, misfortune and sorrow. It separates the upper and lower realms. Acheron is where one could meet Hermes, a messenger of the Gods, upon passing, to be guided onto the ferry to cross over.

Cocytus- The River of waiting, wailing, sound making and heartbreaking distress. This one is cold and punishing. The agony one bears through here is unbearable and undesirable. This energy flows from Acheron.

Lethe- The River of forgetfulness, time, memory and absolution. Forgiveness; like tears washing away the past, flow through you. The breaking point has been overcome and you are starting to draw the water's energy for future use.

Phlegethon- The River of fire, change, truth, light and metamorphous. Here, the water flows into Tartarus, a place of torment for the wicked. This place is hot, transformational, fiery and unrelenting.

Styx-The River of unbreakable promises. This one is named after a deity who has miraculous power to make one invincible. Here also is known to converge into a marsh; also named like this. It is believed that Styx, circles the underworld nine times.

Rivers in Dreams

Take note of the structure of the water in your dream. Is it clear, fresh and making beautiful sound or is there a stormy darkness to it?

Use these energy clues to help yourself to interpret these situations.

Rivers can be metaphors for the blood in our veins; our lives, our energy and our force.

Water is symbolic of mana, emotion and spiritual gifts.

THE STRANGE WORLD BENEATH US
By Paul Dale Roberts, HPI's Esoteric Detective
Halo Paranormal Investigations

When I went to Belize while on my way to Guatemala, I was told to visit the Black Hole Drop. I was told this was the Mother of All Caves. Unfortunately, I did not have the time to visit this cave and had to head out to my final destination. If I could have gone back in time, I would have stayed in Belize, but that is another story. To get to the Black Hole Drop, you hike up the foothills of the Maya Mountains and you will reach the mouth of the cave. This is a very unusual cave. Actun Loch Tunich sinkhole sits over 300 feet above the basin below and 200 feet above the rain forest canopy that grows out from the sinkhole basin.

Reports have come in that UFOs are sighted near the hole and a recent report says that a group of travelers saw a UFO near the mouth of the cave. It was 40 feet long, no wings and had a dome on top. Here is what one witness says: "I have never seen anything like this in my life. We were approaching the Actun Loch Tunich cave to do the Black Hole Drop Tour and we saw this mysterious object just hanging close to the sinkhole and then it moved rapidly unlike any other thing I have ever seen in the air," Steven Williams of Colorado says.

Many visitors to the Black Hole Drop say that it's an adventure you will never forget. You get lowered down through the mouth of the cave. As visitors rappel further downward, they pass the canopy layer and arrive at a deep hole that looks inky black and that is where the name originates from. Special Note: I rappelled down a big hole, it was called Moaning Caverns, an experience I will never forget. Could the Black Hole Drop be a gateway to an underground complex that was created by extraterrestrials? Many abductees have made the claim that their alien abductors have taken them to secret extraterrestrial bases that are underground. Case example: When I went to New Mexico to visit Billy the Kid's Grave with a stopover at Dulce, I was told by locals that they believe there is a jointly operated human and alien underground facility that exists under Archuleta Mesa on the Colorado-New Mexico border near the town of Dulce.

Secret underground complexes are everywhere. Right here in Sacramento, there is a secret passageway from our State Capitol to the California State Library to various other State government facilities. These underground complexes are to be used by our Governor and high officials during a disaster or emergency. Deanna Jaxine Stinson discovered many caverns and caves in her former hometown of Sonora and what she discovered is that most of these caves are extremely haunted by people of the past who temporarily lived in these caves and for past victims of this cave who have actually died in these caves. Many Sonora locals believe that some of the caverns and caves also lead to underground extraterrestrial bases. Why? Because Sonora is in the heart of Gold country and Bill Birnes, a well-

known UFOlogist, made the claim that California's Gold Country is also known as Gold Country UFO Triangle. Many people in Gold Country see strange lights in the sky and strange UFO activity. The theory is that UFOs are attracted to the gold in the Gold Country UFO Triangle. What also is interesting is that UFOs are seen at the Green Valley Vortex and the Green Valley Vortex is in the Gold Country UFO Triangle.

When I visited Area 51 I was told by many locals of Rachel, Nevada that Area 51 has a secret underground complex that leads to many military bases. One local who claimed he worked there at one point says that there is a huge underground base at Area 51 and underground tunnels that lead to Fort Hood, Texas, Fort Huachuca, Arizona, Wright-Patterson AFB, Dulce, New Mexico and at one time Fort Ord, because of the UFO base at Monterey Bay. The former employee of Area 51 says that the tunnels also lead to many other military installations and a black ops government group has complete knowledge of the tunnels. You can see my investigation at Monterey Bay here: sacramentopress.com/2008/11/18/monterey-bay-underground-ufo-base/

If you don't want to be seen, the best place to be is underground. If you want to conduct secretive experiments, the best place to do it is underground. Harold Waters of Los Angeles makes the claim that when he looked into the sewer system in LA, he saw two reptilian humanoids moving about and one of the reptilian creatures looked at him and hissed. Stories abound in LA that reptilians live underneath the city and they come from a UFO base underwater near Catalina Island. When I visited Catalina Island, I was told by a shop keeper that UFOs are often seen near the island. We know what is basically aboveground, but there is so much to explore underneath our Earth and in our oceans and waterways.

FOR MORE INFORMATION:
www.cryptic916.com/
Sacramento Paranormal Help
www.facebook.com/HaloParanormalInvestigations/
Email: jazmaonline@gmail.com
Sacramento Paranormal Haunted Hotline: 916 203 7503

Paul Dale Roberts

OUR HOLLOW EARTH

GIANTS IN THE EARTH:
THE OLYMPIANS,
KINGS OF THE UNDERWORLD
An Olympian Exploration
of Heaven and Hell
By Hercules Invictus

PUBLISHER'S NOTE: — According to Inner Earth theorists, hell may be an actual place. You might want to pass it by on your way to the center of the Earth, but the idea of a real Hades has captivated the "imagination" since such revelations - Biblical or otherwise - were recorded. Join our friend Hercules as he sets forth on a personal odyssey taking him to the Underworld of Greek "mythology." A real journeyman he is indeed!

Hear me, powerful Hercules untamed and strong,
to whom great deeds and mighty works belong!
Strong-man hero, helpful and benign,
of various forms eternal and divine,
throughout the ages, thou has earned our praise,
for thy protective, fierce and manly ways.
A champion, in many arts well skilled,
the avatar of human life fulfilled,
'tis thine, good victor, heroes to empower,
and ward oppressors off with thy stern glower.

By Hercules Invictus
Inspired by Thomas Taylor's 1792
English translation of "The Hymns of Orpheus"

OUR HOLLOW EARTH

THE GOLDEN GIANTS

My eyes are closed and my breathing is now both deep and slow. I am lying in bed, comfortable and warm. The lights have long been extinguished and I feel blissfully peaceful and totally relaxed. Each breath draws me further inwards.

I have navigated through the choppy beta brain waves to nearby alpha, where stillness reigns supreme. I then continue onwards to the misty and mysterious waters of delta. Usually I lose focus (and awareness) at this point and swiftly drift into Hypnos' Realm of Sleep and Dream. Today I manage to stay awake and smoothly enter the hypnogogic state, where existence is much more vivid and malleable than what we experience while awake.

Here the distinction between inner and outer realities no longer exists. What replaces it is a sense of overlapping levels of awareness. And we seem to be present, in one form or another, on all of them simultaneously.

Once localized as a unit of awareness, I navigate unerringly, without thought, trusting my Intent to take me where I need to be.

Almost immediately I find myself in an enclosed oval area whose details are obscured by a blinding white light. A Golden Giant awaits me. I have been here before and no doubt will return here again. This one is male, lean and angular, more than half again my height and clad in long golden robes elaborately embroidered with gold thread. He has an elongated skull, a feature not shared by all of his kind.

The Golden Giants walked among us when Kronos ruled the Earth, during the Reign of the Titans (remembered in our legends as the Age of Gold). After a bloody civil war, which still reverberates through our terrestrial mythologies, some of the Golden Giants migrated to the planet Neptune, an Olympian paradise. Others were exiled to Venus, whose surface can best be described as hellish. A few remained to protect and guide some of us to the realization that we too may be Golden Giants, ensnared in the Dream of Mortality. Those who remained are said to dwell deep below the ground, high up above the clouds and/or deep within our own psyches. They still inspire and communicate through modern myths, including the Shaver Mystery, where they are known as the helpful Teros.

During the course of our repeated interactions I have been informed that the long separated Golden Giants of Neptune, Venus and Earth have finally reconciled their age-old differences and have now banded together to awaken Those Who Sleep.

Presumably, once the stragglers have been gathered, all will be translated to a much better place on another plane and/or planet.

This Golden One, like most of his kind, communicates telepathically. He greets me cheerfully and then asks if I have completed the Tasks I volunteered for when we last met. Some part of me seems to know him and answers (without fully understanding consciously what I am talking about) that all have already been anchored.

He seems content with my answer. He also seems to be focusing on some device that I understand gives him access to my thoughts and memories as we speak.

After a brief pause he informs me that I have not successfully connected with the Underworld and that this must be rectified immediately if our Mission is to succeed.

Though not enthusiastic, I know the drill and am prepared for it. As in a dream or astral journey, I soon find myself hovering above a powerful masculine figure. I know that I am seeing myself, not as I now am but as I once was and, on some level, as I will always be. For time and space, as we understand it while awake, does not exist here either.

My disembodied consciousness enters the figure. I know, with certainty, that I am now the Theban Hercules, son of Zeus and progenitor of my line. I will tackle this challenge as the Highest aspect of my totality as an individuated being. How can I not succeed?

KATABASIS: THE DESCENT

For my final Labor, King Eurystheus charged me with fetching Hades' hound, triple-headed Kerveros. In order to purify me for this task, for no one who is impure can traffic with the Gods Below, the goddess Demeter herself inspired her initiates at Eleusis to institute a new holy rite to honor her daughter Persephone. Through my participation in this rite I would be cleansed of all accrued miasma and rendered pure.

Theseus, the King of Athens, declared me an honorary citizen to facilitate the process of my initiation as Eumolpus, the Hierophant, is a staunch traditionalist and will not initiate foreigners.

It helps that Musaeos, the son of my fellow Argonaut Orpheus, is one of the mystes in attendance. He has prepared me as thoroughly as his Order allows. I have fasted and bathed in the river Illisos. Barefoot, and with my eyes to the ground, I await to be summoned by the white robed officiants, who are now chanting. In my right hand I hold a small piglet by its back legs. In my left hand are some round and sticky cakes. The sweet smell of poppies, both living and dried, the latter offered as incense, permeates the air.

Through this rite I will learn many things that I can never share with the profane, for the secrets of Eleusis are sacrosanct.

To pass the time, I reflect upon what little I already know:

Throughout the known world there are many entrances to the Underworld. For this adventure I will utilize the one on Cape Tenairon, the southernmost point of mainland Hellas. Hades' realm can be accessed through a small cave below the Nekromanteion, where people perform necromantic rituals to coax oracular utterances from the dead.

It is said that when one who is loved by Olympus leaves this world, Hermes, the Divine Herald, or sometimes Thanatos, the Titan of Death, is dispatched to escort him to Hades' realm. All others must find their own way to the nearest portal, descend into the earth's cold bosom, and wait by the banks of the first great river they encounter, either the Styx or the Acheron.

At the moment of death, souls enter Erebus, an in-between realm that bridges and extends into our world, the Underworld and the Dream Realm of Hypnos, Lord of Sleep. If the traditional rites have been observed by family and friends, the deceased can board Charon's Ferry when it arrives and pay the fare of one silver obolus. If not, they must remain in the terrestrial section of Erebus on this side of the river, sometimes for several hundred years. These unhappy souls are claimed by Hekate and often haunt those who neglected their burial rites.

I knew that both Orpheus and Psyche were granted passage by the ferryman while they still drew breath. Would Charon dare deny the son of Zeus the same courtesy? I am confident that he would not.

Those who manage the crossing are herded on the shore and directed to a narrow passageway guarded by Kerveros. The monstrous hound's task is to prevent their leaving his master's kingdom. As it would be impolite of me to steal Hades' dog and Charon's boat on this adventure, I must proceed to my uncle's palace in Erebos on the other side of the rivers and ask for his permission to fulfill Eurystheus' decree. I would not want the winged Erinyes, also known as Furies, loosed upon me at Labor's end.

Psyche, who returned from Hades' realm intact and was reunited with Eros, her true love, once told me that all souls who enter the narrow passageway eventually emerge in the courtyard of Hades' palace, where they are judged by three wise men.

Most souls are assigned to the Asphodel Fields, deprived of all memory. Whenver they thirst, they drink from the nearby river Lethe, which erases their memories anew.

Those who have offended Olympus are sent to Tartarus and assigned torturous punishments. Sisyphus is doomed to roll a large boulder up a steep hill, only to have it roll back down when his task seems accomplished. Tantalus, immersed in water up to his neck beneath a canopy of grape-filled vines a hand-span higher than his head, forever thirsts and hungers. The fifty Danaids must work at filling a far-away pool with cracked clay jars. Ixion, the father of all centaurs, is fastened to a burning wheel that is forever spinning.

OUR HOLLOW EARTH

In Greek mythology, Cerberus was the Hound of Hell who guarded the Underworld.

Complete with poisonous vapors, this is said to be an entrance to hell found in Turkey, but which is part of the ancient Greek culture.

Giants clash in ancient Greece.

A giant footprint. If the "person" that belongs to this is guarding the Underworld, then what chance do we have of going?

OUR HOLLOW EARTH

Heroes, thrice-born mystics and the truly blessed earn a place in Elysium, a beautiful paradise full of endless delights. Each is granted experiences that fulfill their every pleasure. The Garden of the Hesperides, in the far West, is said to be a pale reflection of Elysium's splendor.

The Heroes continue to serve their former human communities in times of great need. Their tombs are well-maintained, sacrificial rites are routinely performed and the holy serpents who dwell in their resting place are treated with the greatest honor and respect.

Only a few souls, those of super-human accomplishment, are granted Olympian status and immortalized in the starry Heavens. In living memory, only Dionysus and Psyche eventually earned this honor.

I idly wonder where my soul will one day reside, but not for long.

Musaeos approaches holding a large square of white cloth. Though solemn in demeanor, his eyes smile at me. He bids me to follow him.

ANABASIS: RE-EMERGING FROM GAIA'S WOMB

As stated, one can never share with non-initiates what was learned or what transpired during the rites of Eleusis. The process is sacred and the realizations have been kept secret and safe since the process was first established during the Age of Heroes.

But I can certainly reinforce some Underworld understandings that I have already encountered in the public domain:

_ Undergoing the rites will profoundly redefine your understanding of Death and Rebirth.

_ You will no longer fear this natural process that all must one day face.

_ You are transformed by the experience of true Initiation.

_ The Underworld can be entered through terrestrial caves, caverns and other openings in the Earth, some natural and some hand-wrought. Ultimately the journey continues beyond the confines of the physical plane.

_ If you know how you can access the Underworld directly via other planes of being and states of mind.

_ Once you have entered the Underworld, a part of you will always remain there. In Greek Mythology, Odysseus encountered the shade of the Theban Hercules hunting the shade of Medusa. Both shades were stuck in this pointless drama.

_ Kerveros, Hades' three headed canine, is tasked with preventing individuals from leaving the Underworld. He accomplishes this through fear. Aside from his great size and many heads, Kerveros' fur is riddled with venomous snakes (like Medusa's crown). To conquer him you must fully face your fears, both large and small.

OUR HOLLOW EARTH

_ The Underworld will teach you many uncomfortable but undeniable truths.

_ Visiting the Underworld extends an invitation for the Underworld's denizens to visit you.

_ Heaven and Hell are states of mind as well as Underworld locations. You can readily experience the reality of Heaven and Hell while you still draw breath.

_ The Golden Giants are indeed present in the Underworld and play an active role in attempting to free the kin some of them once imprisoned in the bodies and minds of mortals. They can be called upon to protect their lost sons and daughters as much as they can from detrimental (Dero) influences that might otherwise target them.

_ Wisdom from the East: Thou art That.

_ And as Hermes the Thrice-Great once said: As above, so below. As within, so without.

Onwards!

(c) Hercules Invictus

OUR HOLLOW EARTH

IS THERE A HOLLOW EARTH
JOHN F. KENNEDY
ASSASSINATION CONNECTION?

By Sean Casteel

*** Admiral Richard E. Byrd is thought of as an iconic American hero. But what was he concealing from the public, and why did he swear to secrecy a handpicked group from among the crews that accompanied him on his polar expeditions?

*** In 1938, the Nazis asked Byrd to join their expedition to the North Pole, which the admiral quite naturally declined. The Nazis went there without him, seeking to make contact with a hidden race of supermen by finding a doorway into the Hollow Earth that was believed to exist in the icy northern wastelands. Did the Nazis succeed in making that contact? Did they get alien assistance in building their own disc-shaped aircraft?

*** The admiral's cousin, David Harold Byrd, was an oil-rich financier from Texas who funded some of Admiral Byrd's earlier polar expeditions. By virtue of his wealth, Harold Byrd was part of the inner circle of the wealthy and powerful in Texas, which included Lyndon Johnson and John Connelly. Did the secret cabal somehow have a hand in the assassination of John F. Kennedy? Was the conspiracy of murder birthed in a Houston hotel room?

*** There is said to be a world beneath our feet, a civilization located at the innermost core of our planet. Some call it the Hollow Earth or the Inner Earth. It has been described as a virtual paradise by some and a horrifying, hellish nightmare by others. Doorways into this mystery realm have been sought for centuries, but has the actual opening been photographed from space by our modern day satellites?

****

OUR HOLLOW EARTH

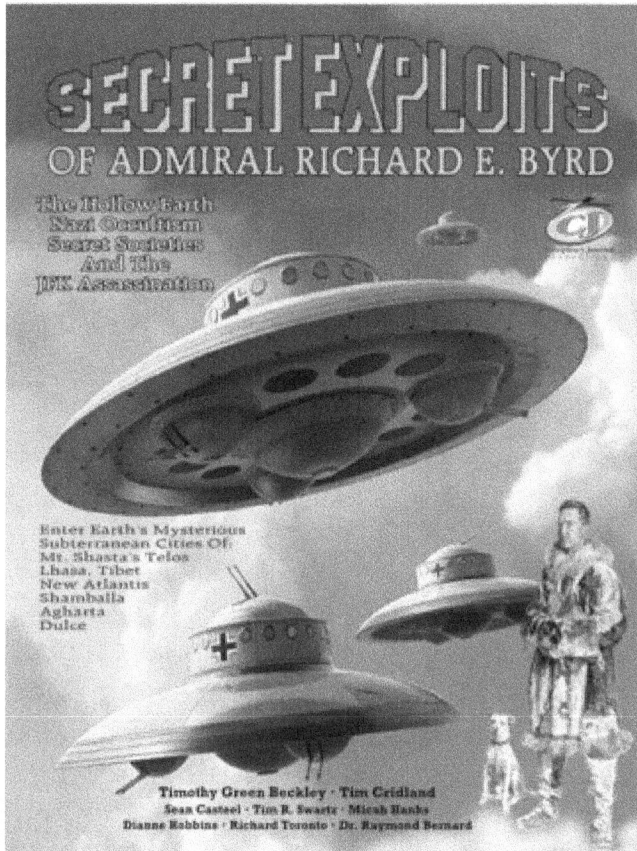

The latest book from publisher Timothy Beckley investigates a possible Hollow Earth/UFO/JFK assassination connection.

TO many in the UFO and conspiracy theory communities, Admiral Richard E. Byrd is not merely some benign fatherly figure smiling at us from the pages of 20th century history. While Byrd is commonly thought of as a national hero and a courageous explorer of the forbidding wastelands of the Polar Regions, those who look a little deeper soon discover a disturbing darkness and subterfuge that entangles the American icon in many a wicked web.

The history of Byrd's covert "dance with the demons" is covered most thoroughly in a 2017 book issued by Global Communications/ Conspiracy Journal, Timothy Green Beckley's publishing house. The book is called "Secret Exploits of Admiral Richard E. Byrd," and is subtitled "The Hollow Earth, Nazi Occultism, Secret Societies and the JFK Assassination." Beckley uses his usual "kitchen sink" method, employing several writers who attack the various subjects from a great many angles.

THE STORY OF BYRD AS AN EXPLORER BEGINS

In the interest of disclosure, I also contributed a few chapters to "Secret Exploits of Admiral Richard E. Byrd," including a Q and A with Tim R. Swartz, Beckley's resident expert on all things Byrd.

"Before he was Admiral Byrd," Swartz told me, "he was Richard Evelyn Byrd, Jr. and he was born in 1888. Byrd graduated from the Naval Academy in 1912 and was commissioned an Ensign in the U.S. Navy. He volunteered to become a naval aviator."

Along with a keen interest in flying, Byrd also had a fascination with exploration. By the time he came of age, there was little new left in the world to explore except the Polar Regions. Expeditions had been traveling to the areas at the North and South Poles since the 19th century, but Byrd believed he could do a more complete job of exploring there, especially with the added advantage of aircraft that would give his team the ability to view the icy regions from the sky.

OUR HOLLOW EARTH

Admiral Byrd and fellow pilot Floyd Bennett, the team that flew over the North Pole.

"His first trip was in 1926," Swartz said, "when, along with a pilot named Floyd Bennett, he attempted to fly over the North Pole in a tri-motor monoplane. It lasted about fourteen to fifteen hours, and they claimed to have reached the North Pole, covering a distance of about 1,500 miles. They encircled it and then managed to make it back safely. When he returned to the U.S., he was a national hero. Congress even passed a special act that promoted him to the rank of commander and awarded him the National Medal of Honor. From that point on, to the U.S., Byrd could do no wrong."

In 1938, Byrd visited Nazi Germany. The Nazis were intent on exploring the Arctic themselves and invited Byrd to participate in their expedition. Times being what they were politically, Byrd quite naturally declined. So the Nazis went to the North Pole without him and probably established several bases in the region, beginning then and lasting through the duration of World War II, according to Swartz.

THE MYSTERY OF 'HIGHJUMP,' THE ABORTED MISSION

Operation Highjump

In 1946, in postwar America, Operation Highjump was conceived. Intended to be an exploratory visit of Antarctica, the huge number of ships, helicopters and other aircraft, along with 4,000 personnel, that were mustered for the project continues to arouse suspicion. Although the expedition was originally planned to last for six months, the mission was called off after only three weeks, with the team claiming they had done all the exploring necessary.

OUR HOLLOW EARTH

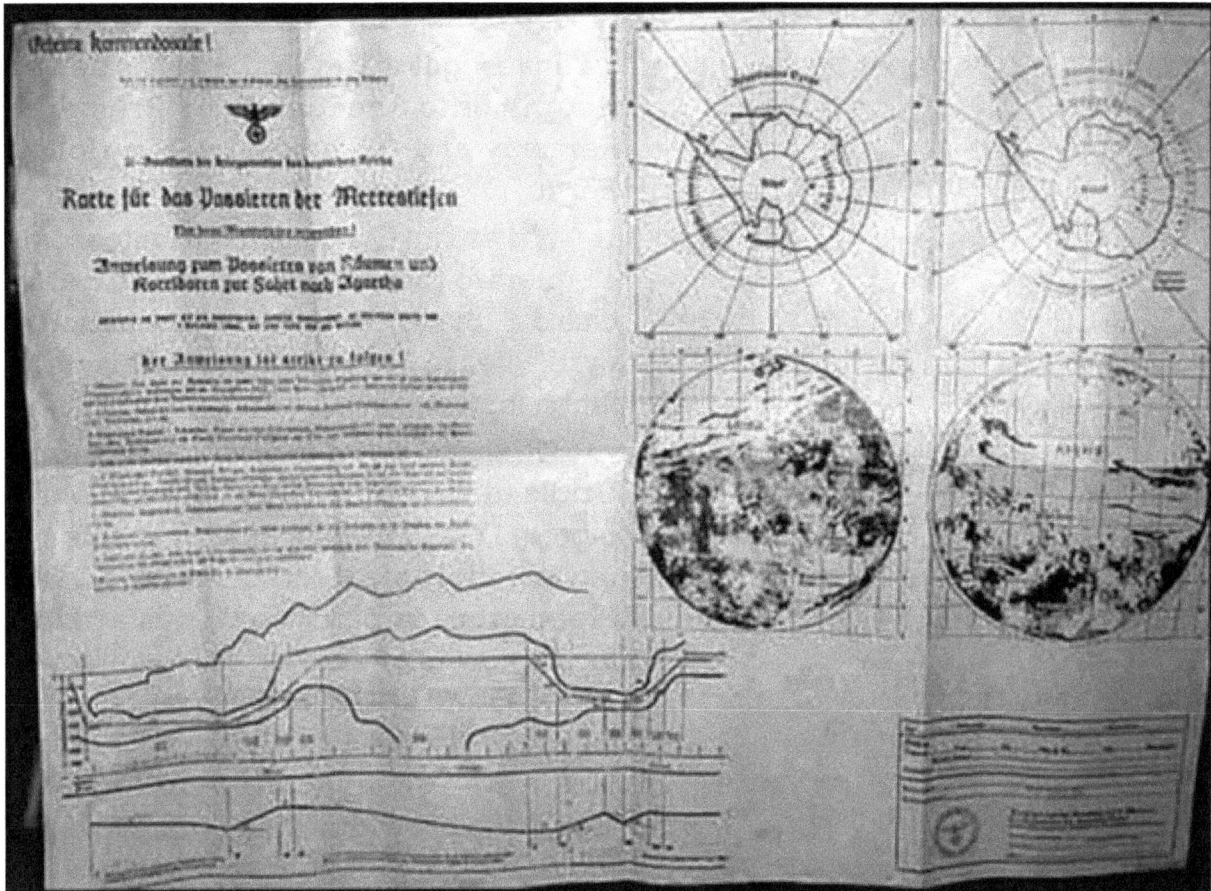

The Nazis were intensely interested in exploring the South Pole and even drew up maps which some say pinpointed the location of an opening to the inside of the Earth.

"Some people have speculated," Swartz said, "that they went there in search of a secret Nazi base hidden somewhere along the coast of Antarctica. At the end of World War II, there were a number of German U-boats that had left the Canary Islands carrying personnel, equipment, supplies and things like that. They would later surrender in Argentina but without all the personnel and equipment on board. Now, one of the U-boat captains said that they had dropped off their people, equipment, etc. at a secret base in Antarctica. And declassified documents show that this could be one of the reasons why this expedition Operation Highjump had been established, to find out just what was going on in Antarctica."

Swartz said that the Nazis had become interested in places like Antarctica because Hitler believed there might be an entrance there that would lead into the Hollow Earth. According to the occult lore that Hitler subscribed to, the Hollow Earth was the home of the Root Race, the Aryan people, supermen that Hitler hoped would aid him in his dream of world conquest.

OUR HOLLOW EARTH

FREEMASONRY, SECRECY AND THE 'LOYAL LEGION'

Investigator Tim Cridland has delved deeply into the death of President Kennedy and the existence of a Hollow Earth.

Writer Tim Cridland contributes some chapters to "Secret Exploits of Admiral Richard E. Byrd," including a discussion of Byrd's ties to Freemasonry and his reputation for secrecy.

"Richard Byrd was a Freemason," Cridland writes, "having joined a Washington, D.C., lodge in 1921. It seems being members of secret societies – and the Freemasons in particular – was a 'thing' for explorers of the day. The mainly volunteer crew at Little America, the base camp for Byrd's 1928 Antarctic expedition, were so unruly that Byrd formed a secret society within the group. Eleven of the 42 men at the base were Masons like Byrd. Byrd's secret society, which he called the 'Loyal Legion,' was obviously based on the Masonic systems of initiation and confidentiality."

Byrd, in order to protect himself from mutiny in Antarctica and to guard his reputation when he returned to the U.S., made the initiates swear to divulge to no one the existence of the Loyal Legion. They further had to swear that they would not try to learn the names of other members of the group. Most importantly, they swore to do whatever Byrd asked them to do and not to tell anyone that Byrd asked them to do it.

"If Byrd needed people around him that were loyal and able to keep secrets," Cridland explains, "and he found Freemasonry to be a system that facilitated this, his future actions were congruous. On his next Antarctic expedition, which took place in 1934-35, 60 of the 82 members were Freemasons. He established the First Antarctic Lodge, number 777, in February of 1935."

It does seem as though Byrd was stacking the deck by surrounding himself with like-minded Freemasons who were willing to keep his secrets both inside and outside the lodge. Just the sort of thing that conspiracy theorists, such as ourselves, tend to find significant.

OUR HOLLOW EARTH

IS THERE PHOTOGRAPHIC PROOF OF THE HOLLOW EARTH?

Cridland also contributes a chapter about the "Hole-at-the-Pole Theory," the same allegedly supernatural portal that had sent the Nazis scurrying to find a way into the Hollow Earth.

"The question most often asked by the uninitiated," Cridland writes, "when discussing the Hollow Earth theory: 'If there are holes at the poles, why aren't there any satellite photos of them?' The usual response is to pull out the photos uncovered by Ray Palmer in the June 1970 issue of 'Flying Saucers Magazine.' Palmer, the man that some claim was responsible for starting the public's obsession with flying saucers, had started the modern-day Hollow Earth movement in an earlier issue of the magazine.

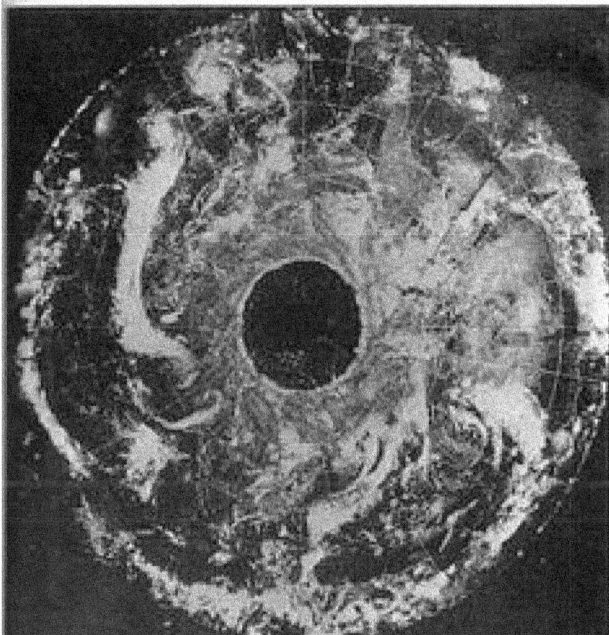

Photo purports to show opening at the North Pole.

"Palmer, upon finding the photo taken by the ESSA-7 satellite on November 23, 1968, declared 'The North Pole photo, lacking clouds in the polar area, therefore reveals the surface of the planet. Although surrounding the polar area, and north of such areas as the North American continent and Greenland and the Asian continent, we can see the ice fields of the eight-foot thick ice. But in the photo, we do not see any ice fields in a large circular area directly at the geographic pole. Instead, we see – THE HOLE!'"

But Palmer's claims have been impossible to verify with follow-up photos. Cridland says that is likely because there have been a scant few other photos that claimed to show a polar void, and that even fewer are taken from a polar-orbiting satellite. Which makes photos relevant to this discussion hard to find. Later photos, which captured images using the relatively new capability of infrared satellite photography and taken long after Palmer's enthusing over the 1968 satellite photo, did not prove the existence of the hole either. The expected heat signature of the supposed hole simply wasn't there.

Cridland says this does not mean we should rule out the possibility of a Hollow Earth, however, since we are dealing with government photos that may have been doctored before being released to the public. We are already aware of a longstanding cover-up by the government as regards UFOs and the "aliens" who occupy them, so it requires no great leap of faith to believe this kind of secrecy may apply to the Hollow Earth as well.

BYRD'S COUSIN AND THE HOUSTON HOTEL ROOM CONSPIRACY

Speaking of government cover-ups, Cridland also contributes a chapter to "Secret Exploits of Admiral Richard E. Byrd" that closely examines the relationship between the admiral and his cousin as well as a strange connection to the assassination of John F. Kennedy.

"Byrd's cousin, David Harold Byrd," Cridland writes, "was instrumental in funding Byrd's polar expeditions before the government took over. Harold Byrd promoted the expeditions quite literally like carnival attractions, having a replica of the Antarctic base Little America set up at the 1936 Texas Centennial Exposition. Richard Byrd showed his appreciation by naming an Antarctic mountain range after his cousin and benefactor.

David Harold Byrd

"Harold Byrd's oil wealth," Cridland continues, "granted him entry into the inner circle of Texas power. He was a member of the 8F group, an elite organization named after the room number of the Lamar Hotel in Houston where they held meetings. The group of predominately right-wing business men had Lyndon Johnson and John Connelly in its ranks. 8F also coordinated political activities with other Southern right-wing politicians and businessmen, including Billie Sol Estes and Clint Murchison. These are names that are very familiar to researchers who have investigated Lyndon Johnson's connections to the JFK assassination."

Cridland sketches in further damning details, such as the fact that Harold Byrd was the owner of the Texas School Book Depository, the building that Lee Harvey Oswald worked at and the alleged location of the fatal shots. Harold Byrd bought the building in 1939. When he returned from a suspiciously-timed, two-month Af-

OUR HOLLOW EARTH

rican safari in January of 1964, Harold Byrd had the window that Oswald allegedly fired from – the window of the sniper's nest – removed and kept it as a souvenir.

"He morbidly decorated the bottom half of the window with newspaper clippings of the assassination," Cridland writes, "and postcard pictures of Kennedy, Dealey Plaza and his Book Depository. He framed it and put it in the banquet room of his mansion, where it remained until the day he died in 1986."

It is as though Harold Byrd took no small amount of covert pride in the fact that he was part of both the successful presidential assassination and the subsequent – and quite nearly impenetrable – cover-up. While there is no obvious direct link between the Admiral himself and the purported Texas-based conspiracy, his blood relationship with his deep-pocketed cousin Harold should raise a few flags of interest. If the long and tangled thread of subterfuge and collusion that surrounds the JFK assassination is ever publicly exposed, will it be possible to follow the thread back to a Houston hotel room and the oil-rich David Harold Byrd?

MICAH HANKS ON THE NAZI CONNECTION

From the darkness surrounding Byrd, his cousin and the JFK assassination, we move along to what may be even darker terrain, as described by author and podcaster Micah Hanks.

"It's one of the most famous conspiracies," Hanks writes, "associated with the end of the Second World War: that a group of Nazis escaped to Antarctica, where they had a secret base established to aid in the furtherance of their top secret flying saucer development program. Such tales have been the stuff of legends for decades now, and the persistence of rumors like these offer an alternative to popular theories about alien visitors that remain a hallmark of modern UFO lore."

Hanks refers to a 2006 discovery by Ohio State University scientists who claim to have located some kind of "gravitation anomaly" located below Wilkes Land, Antarctica. It was later speculated in the tabloid press that the anomaly could be the long-sought "secret Nazi UFO base" in question.

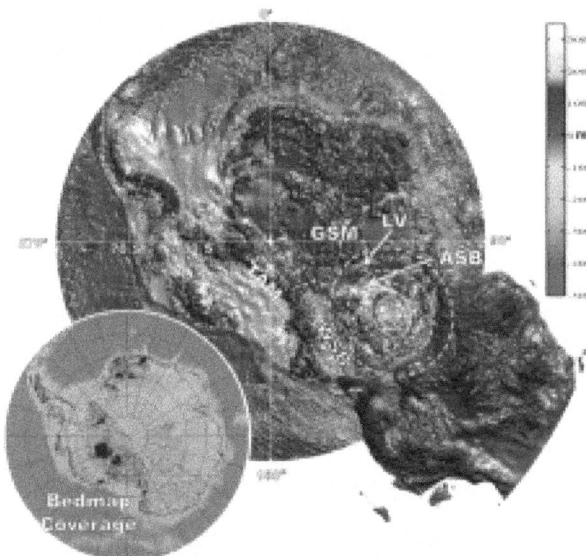

"Gravitational anomaly" located below Wilkes Land, Antarctica.

There is some legitimacy to this idea, according to Hanks, stemming from the fact that the Nazis did mount an expedition to the South Pole in 1938-39, though there is no proof they attempted to establish a more permanent stronghold there. Ironically, according to Hanks, the idea of Nazi UFOs in Antarctica has less to do with anything the Nazis actually did

57

than with what Admiral Byrd himself said about it.

Hanks quotes from a 1947 interview with Byrd, published in a Chilean newspaper, thusly: "The admiral stated that he didn't want to frighten anyone unduly but that it was a bitter reality that, in case of a new war, the continental United States would be attacked by flying objects which could fly from pole to pole at incredible speeds."

"As one can see," Hanks continues, "such wording easily lends itself to the idea of a connection between the Nazi UFO mythos and something going on at the South Pole."

Yet the answer is still not so simple, according to Hanks. But we'll leave the rest of what he has to say to readers of "Secret Exploits of Admiral Richard E. Byrd," who will no doubt approve Hanks' thorough research and attempt to document the truth about a conspiracy theory that so far shows no sign of being abandoned.

THE TIP OF THE PROVERBIAL ICEBERG

"Secret Exploits of Admiral Richard E. Byrd" also includes the contributions of other writers, like Dianne Robbins, Richard Toronto and Dr. Raymond Bernard.

Among the chapters I wrote myself is one about the legends of "Agharta," a paradise located in the Hollow Earth that is lit by a wondrous internal sun and is sometimes visited by spiritual seekers of truth, like the reincarnated Buddhist monk, T. Lobsang Rampa. I also write about the Hollow Earth as described by writer Richard Shaver, who says the interior of our planet is a virtual infernal hell occupied by a demonic race he calls the "dero," who use their ancient technology to wreak a continual evil havoc on us surface dwellers.

"Secret Exploits of Admiral Richard E. Byrd" runs that gamut between the extremes of heaven and hell even as it places the often secretive Admiral – and various related conspiracies and secret societies – firmly in the context of known American history. The obvious Polar Regions pun is this: We are only seeing the tip of a dark and mysterious iceberg so far and must wait to learn whatever truth is ultimately revealed about Byrd and the secrets he so closely guarded.

OUR HOLLOW EARTH

Sean Casteel

SUGGESTED READING:

SECRET EXPLOITS OF ADMIRAL RICHARD E. BYRD: THE HOLLOW EARTH, NAZI OCCULTISM, SECRET SOCIETIES AND THE JFK ASSASSINATION

THE SECRET LOST DIARY OF ADMIRAL RICHARD E. BYRD AND THE PHANTOM OF THE POLES

THE SMOKY GOD AND OTHER INNER EARTH MYSTERIES – UPDATED/EXPANDED EDITION

NAZI UFO TIME TRAVELERS

OUR YOUTUBE CHANNEL – MR. UFO'S SECRET FILES (OVER 400 VIDEOS)

https://www.youtube.com/user/MRUFO1100

OUR HOLLOW EARTH

8

SEARCHING FOR LATIN AMERICAN ENTRANCES TO THE UNDERWORLD
By Scott Corrales
(c) 2019

Although it may not be politically correct to say so, the wonders of Mayan civilization are tinged with more than a bit of horror: grim deities, felines with dreadful fangs and the ever-present reality of human sacrifice. This darkness extended beyond the fantastic, foreboding ruins that the Mayas bequeathed us and into the realm of their religious beliefs.

Mayan cosmology included a particularly unpleasant underground location: a city ruled by Hun-Camé and Vucub-Camé, literally "One Death" and "Many Deaths," the lords of Xibalbá, the underworld. Their rule also extended to diseases that tormented surface dwellers. Like all underworlds of myth, it was unpleasant - a region of twisting, downward roads and underground rivers, filled with thorns and places for torturing unwary travelers, in a manner reminiscent of Richard Shaver's mythic "Deros."

It is not necessary to go into the struggles of surface heroes against the lords of the underworld, captured by the Popol Vuh. Suffice it to say that the belief persisted for years that access to Xibalbá was actually possible by entering cave systems in the vicinity of the Guatemalan city of Cobán - not at all unlikely when we consider that nearly ten percent of the Central American country contains fascinating caverns.

Subterranean cities and temples played a major role in pre-European Latin American societies: religious rites of all kinds were held in these underground locations and tradition holds they were used as warehouses for the storage of treasure and forgotten lore. Still other traditions hold that these underground facilities were not built by the civilizations to which historians and archaeologists usually ascribe their provenance, but by ancient "elder races," whose only remains can be found in mysterious megalithic constructions around the world.

OUR HOLLOW EARTH

A PERUVIAN UNDERWORLD

Dr. Raul Rios Centeno of Peru's INDECOPI organization formed part of a six-man team (five researchers and a guide) who braved the dizzying altitudes of the Andes to go in search of La Chincana, the subterranean city located beneath the former Inca capital of Cuzco.

On July 15, 1998, after undergoing a brief acclimatization period to the 3500 meter elevation of Cuzco, Dr. Rios's team met up with Inez Puente de la Vega, a historian whose knowledge of Inca culture and command of the Runa-Simi variant of the Quechua language would prove of great help in their expedition.

The group's initial efforts focused on finding a point of access to the fabled Chincana: locals informed them that one of the main entrances to the underground city was precisely beneath the Sacsayhuaman archaeological fortress — whose giant stonework is pre-Inca in origin — about a kilometer away from Cuzco. Other sources hinted at the existence of two other gateways: one in the Koricancha or Palace of the Sun, which was partially demolished during the Colonial period to build the Carmelite Monastery, and still another beneath Cuzco's great cathedral.

Not surprisingly, scholars at the University of San Antonio de Abad and the Andean University, both of them in Cuzco, refused to speak to the explorers about the putative underground city. But as chance would have it, the Rios party managed to gain access to the Andean University's library, where a fascinating piece of information was uncovered.

In 1952, a group of twelve explorers—a mixed group of French and American researchers—managed to gain access through the Sacsayhuaman entrance with enough provisions to last for five days as they embarked upon what they termed "the greatest discovery since Machu Picchu."

The team ventured into the Sacsayhuaman entrance and nothing further was heard from them until fifteen days later, when French explorer Phillipe Lamontierre emerged from the hole suffering from acute dementia and with visible signs of malnourishment and even the bubonic plague (attributable, says Dr. Rios, to the bats inhabiting the underground spaces). The broken survivor indicated that his fellow adventurers had died, and some of them had even fallen down unfathomed abysses. Among his belongings was an ear of corn made of solid gold, which was later entrusted to the Cuzco Museum of Archaeology (no indication is given as to whether it is on display or not).

While sobered by the Lamontierre experience, Dr. Rios' group resolutely asked the National Institute of Culture's authorization to enter the depths at their own risk, and requesting that the concrete plug covering the entrance be demolished. Officialdom turned a deaf ear to this plea, and the group had to find more devious ways of accomplishing its objectives.

OUR HOLLOW EARTH

Having given "valuable consideration" to the security guards at Sacsayhuaman, the Rios group managed to get into one of the connecting chambers to the underground complex. Equipped with infrared goggles, the group penetrated a chamber that measured scarcely 1.13 meters from the door's stone frame to the rocky floor. "The stench within the [connecting chamber]," writes Dr. Rios, "was nauseating, as it had been employed as a latrine for some time. For some strange reason, the stonework did not reflect infrared rays. However, with the aid of our friend Jorge Zegarra, we were able to apply a RAD-2 X-ray filter, which provided a radio-opacity of 400 to 600% that of aluminum."

"It was thus that we reached a hallway whose height progressively diminished until reaching a scant 94 centimeters," continues his letter. "and given that our average height is 1.80 meters, we had no choice but to return to our starting point."

The Rios party tried to obtain readings on their Geiger counter without much success, but through the RAD-2 X-ray filter, they managed to secure a number of photos which led them to the conclusion that "a coating of some dense metal"— comparable to lead—existed within the hallways, and that there were cracks in the stonework which indeed allowed for the passage of X-rays. At this point, the guide abandoned the mission out of a very real fear of reprisals by the Culture Institute.

Dr. Rios concludes his letter by saying that the images captured by means of the RAD-2 device were being analyzed by Carlos Garcia and Guillermo LaRosa Richardson of the School of Engineering in Lima, Peru. Jacques Bergier was of the opinion that the theory of said subterranean realms was not absurd a priori, but there was no evidence to substantiate such claims, and that "surprises may be in store in this area." The archaeologist's shovel and fortuitous discoveries by laymen have added to the knowledge accumulated over the decades in this field.

Before dismissing these claims out of hand, the Spanish chronicler De Cieza, in describing the wealth and might of the Inca Empire, suggested that much of the royal treasure—and population—had been taken to an underground fastness in the Andes. Treasure hunters have sought the entrances to this purported Inca stronghold over the centuries, occasionally giving rise to stories of "passages lined with gold leaf" and forgotten castles in the Peruvian Amazon. Erich Von Daniken wrote about such passages in The Gold of the Gods, but subsequently disclaimed having seen them in person. In March 1972, Serge Debru, posthumously decorated with France's prestigious Order of Merit, set out to find these subterranean Inca dwellings, never to return. He stated on a taped message: "I know where I'm going and I also know that no one has gone there yet. I shall reveal the secrets of my journey upon my return." After a seventeen day search, rescue parties were unable to find any trace of Debru's expedition. It was later asserted that Debrú was slain by members of the Machihuenga tribe, who freely admitted their wrongdoing to Yoshiharu Sekino, an explorer of the Amazonian Basin.

American explorer John Perkins may have found the entrance to the underground realm that Debru sought: he followed the course of a river that plunged below the surface into colossal caverns lit by greenish light issuing from strange, unclassified vegetation.

The truth of the matter is that South America, and indeed, most continents, appear to be riddled with tunnels leading far and deep toward somewhere. Most investigators have turned back when they have encountered either unsurmountable obstructions or tunnels filled with seawater. There is no doubt about the artificial nature of this phenomena, or that their creation in the hardest bedrock would have involved either explosives, lasers or chemical means of eroding stone unknown to 20th century science.

The work of another eminent researcher must be mentioned at this point. Daniel Ruzo crafted an elaborate interpretation of the Biblical Flood, supposedly based on his discoveries in Latin America. According to Ruzo, antediluvian humankind was very advanced and quite aware of the impending cataclysm - much in the same way that our civilization is aware of destructive solar flares and encroaching ice ages. Ruzo posited that Noah was simiply one of many 'patriarchs' selected to preserve human life and knowledge, but adding the detail that the 'ark', far from being a seagoing concern, was really a cavern. Arguing that no known vessel could have withstood the tremendous waves sweeping the globe, and the ark should be understood as something that contains or encompasses something. The biblical measurements are better suited to a cave than a ship.

In his book La Historia Fantástica de un Descubrimiento (The Fantastic Story of a Discovery), Ruzo stated that his theories had their origin in the experiences of his mentor, the occultist Pedro Astete. During the course of a dream, Astete found himself in what he described as a vast underground library filled with scrolls. Suddenly, a voice overwhelmed him with a single word: "Masma." We can assume he promptly woke up in a cold sweat.

Subsequent inquiries proved that the mysterious word received in the dream state was actually the Quechua term that was interchangeably used for a cavern or an inner sanctum of sorts. Further research led the occultist to believe there was a connection between the word heard in his dreams and Northern Africa, and he came upon the notion that the word referred to the Tuareg (or Touareg) people, who somehow came to the Americas via "underground tunnels left over from the age of bright Atlantis." This effort at linguistic anthropology fell well short of the mark, however...the name "Masma" is given to the fifth of twelve children of Isma'il, father of the Fulani peoples (Abu Alfa Umar bin Farid, "The Lost and Found Children of Abraham," p. 116).

Tunnels of Sacsayhuaman in the Andes lead to the Underworld.

Juan Moricz journeyed into a vast tunnel system.

OUR HOLLOW EARTH

Proof of an ancient underground system in South America located by Juan Moricz.

J.J. Benítez, author of over 50 UFO books.

Mexican temple – is it an entrance to an Inner Earth civilization?

OUR HOLLOW EARTH

Astete - and Ruzo - were probably unaware of this detail, but went on to mention an old Nigerian legend about a lengthy tunnel in that African country that extended all the way to Egypt on the one end, and all the way to the sea (the Atlantic Ocean) on the other. Astete extrapolated on this belief to suggest the tunnel "extended to Atlantis, and later to the New World."

BEWARE OF THE "DWELLERS IN THE DEPTHS"

The name of Juan Moricz—a Hungarian nobleman turned Argentinean citizen—stands heads and shoulders above all others in these accounts of subterranean lairs in South America.

Indefatigable author and investigator Magdalena del Amo-Freixedo met Moricz in Ecuador and was able to hear from the late miner/explorer's very lips the story of how he came upon a subterranean realm verging on the fantastic.

Moricz stated that when he was a newly-arrived emigre in Argentina, he ran across an old man who told him about the "lost treasure of Atahualpa" and how it had been concealed by his followers in a series of subterranean cities. Fired by this knowledge, young Moricz decided to cross the breadth of Argentina until he reached the Andes and headed northward to where the mighty South American mountain range gives birth to the Amazon's headwaters.

In a scene straight out of Spielberg's "Raiders of the Lost Ark," Moricz came across tribes of fearsome Jívaro headhunters who are openly hostile to all outsiders. But rather than ending up another shrunken head, he discovered that he could make himself understood to the Jívaros by addressing them in his native Magyar! While this alone might strain anyone's suspension of disbelief, the fact remains that Moricz was able to live among the Jívaros long enough to learn their ways and make an important discovery: the jungle natives had peculiar dotted tattoos across their faces, centered on both cheeks, the chin and the nose. One day, he came across two Jívaro sentries guarding a boulder covered in the same design as the natives wore on their faces. Beyond the rock lay a narrow cave, and the explorer knew that he'd come across the access to the alleged lost hoard.

But the Jívaros cautioned him against entering, stating that the "dwellers in the depths" were gods endowed with beams capable of killing intruders and cutting through stone. The natives insisted on having seen the ground split open and produce brilliant balls of light that would rise heavenward.

Moricz decided that he was willing to place his life in jeopardy merely to see this fabled underground realm. He ventured into the cave, and then down some sort of chimney formation, leading to a slanted corridor made of perfectly dressed, angular stone. His wanderings eventually brought him to a chamber that was "perfectly lit by a quartz column" and from which many other hallways radiated.

Following one of them, Moricz came to a hall with a large circular table of polished stone, surrounded by seven stone seats. The walls were so highly polished as to be mirrored. Dubbing it "The Hall of the Seven Elders," the explorer pressed on, entering a series of narrow hallways which were as filthy as the earlier chambers had been clean. By now tired and forlorn from his meandering in this series of forgotten galleries, he was most startled to come across a cascade of greenish-blue water which appeared to be self-luminous. His heart sank upon realizing that it had reached the end of the tunnels.

Suddenly — he told Del Amo-Freixedo — it occurred to him to go under the cascade and see if anything lay beyond. He was rewarded by brilliant sunlight and a sort of "terrace" looking down at the jungle canopy, hundreds of feet below. A narrow ledge led him to a large flat stone and the urge to "dig under it with his bare hands" to move it. Succeeding in this attempt, he reentered a series of ascending and descending passageways which ended in a vast chamber whose size he estimated at five hundred meters long by four hundred meters wide. The contents of this gargantuan hall — piles of gold, skeletons clad in unusual golden armor — appeared to be its source of illumination.

And it is here where Moricz's already incredible story becomes fantastic: at the end of this "treasure chamber" were five creatures clad in metallic garments and having egg-shaped heads with large slanted black eyes. Their hair was held by an emerald-bearing band. "Your boldness has led you to where you are now," one of them reportedly said. "We have allowed you to reach us."

The creature then expounded on the catastrophes that had destroyed the surface races and how the entire history of their species was kept on gold-leafed books. He was then told to turn back and return to his people, but not to touch anything. "If you do, you will never return to the surface," they cautioned.

Many experts have written off Moricz's exploits as "tall tales" in the best tradition of Baron Munchausen, and cite his collaboration with Erich Von Daniken in "The Gold of the Gods" as proof of Moricz's nearly bottomless "private stock." It is up to the reader to decide.

ASSYRIAN SPELUNKERS IN ANCIENT CENTRAL AMERICA?

But even if we should choose to dismiss the adventures of Juan Moricz as merely fanciful, it by no means discredits the existence of the subterranean galleries.

In 1985, Spain's eminent UFO researcher, J.J. Benítez, joined the late Andreas Faber Kaiser and brothers Carlos and Ricardo Vílchez in exploring a series of clearly artificial tunnels which were not in the Andes, but in the Central American republic of Costa Rica.

According to the story, a Costa Rican family had learned many years ago that there was an ancient tunnel—located on the top of a nameless hill—which very possibly leads to an underground city. The family sold all of its belongings and

OUR HOLLOW EARTH

literally "took to the hills," engaging in amateur excavations which resulted in the discovery of the opening to the tunnel. They found a shaft which dropped almost vertically and constituted the access to a corridor of dressed stone.

Members of the anonymous family group approached investigator Benítez and urged him to take a look. Accompanied by his fellow researchers, Benítez descended by means of a rickety ladder and found himself staring at vast cyclopean blocks—carefully dressed and placed with almost geometric succession. At the end of the gallery, a side wall revealed a curious inscription written in an unknown language.

Subsequent linguistic research by Prof. Jesús Conte revealed that the curious inscription in the forgotten Costa Rican tomb was very similar to ancient Assyrian script [my italics]. Prof. Conte's painstaking analysis disclosed that the characters stated: "Beware! Impending Disaster!"

No good reason has been offered for the discovery of proto-Assyrian text in a cyclopean gallery fifty meters beneath the earth in Costa Rica, thousands of miles from the Middle East. Benítez speculates that this proto-Assyrian may have indeed been the language spoken on Atlantis and which later survived in the Fertile Crescent. If Benítez's suppositions are on target, the reader can well imagine what impeding disaster was being referred to.

Stories of networks of artificially created tunnels riddling the five continents are certainly nothing new: adventure writers of the '30s waxed eloquent on the supposed tunnels in Central Asia which linked a number of cave systems to the mystical realm of Agharta, or the tunnels beneath Lhasa's Potala temple linking it to other lamaseries in the Himalayas; the connectivity between the cave systems of the Rocky Mountains is also well-known.

MORE MEXICAN ODDITIES

Mexico offers its own share of subterranean mysteries. Foremost among these is the "sunken palace" of Dzibilchaltún.

In 1941, a group of teenagers bathing in one of the Yucatan Peninsula's many limestone cenotes, was startled to discover that behind the jungle thickness that surrounded their favorite bathing spot was a wall of dressed stone. They notified the authorities, which in turn advised the Secretariat of Education. Faced with the prospect of cleaning up this twenty square mile area, containing approximately four hundred structures, the Mexican government turned to the Middle American Research Institute at the University of New Orleans, which would in coming years begin exploring the ruins of Dzibilchaltún — the name given by an old Maya shaman, who informed them that the word was not of Mayan origin. However, the lagoon near the ruins had a clearly Mayan denomination: Xlacah, "the old city."

The archaeologists were clearly mystified by this denomination, and suspect-

68

ing that the old shaman was making reference to some sort of acropolis, requested more information. They were then regaled with the story of how in ages past, a massive palace had once occupied the area—the home of Dzibilchaltún's ruler— and how one day a stranger had appeared at the palace gate, requesting shelter. The ruler ordered his servants to prepare lodging for the unexpected guest. The following day, in exchange for the cacique's hospitality, the strange traveler produced a large green gem from his satchel and turned it over to the ruler, who soon turned greedy and asked the stranger if his satchel contained even more treasures. When the stranger refused to answer, he was summarily executed by the guards and the satchel was handed to the ruler, who was disappointed to find in it only some travel-stained garments and a large black stone. In rage, the cacique hurled the black stone out a window: it struck the ground with a tremendous explosion, causing the palace and its occupants to slide into the newly created hole.

It wasn't until 1961 that archaeologists would brave the depths of Xlacah: their exploration of the muddy cenote proved that the limestone structure was shaped like a boot and extended to a depth that was hard to fathom. Upon reaching the end of the vertical segment, they found the remains of the "sunken palace's" columns and adorned walls.

ARGENTINA'S UNDERGROUND CITY

Subterranean cities built by "Atlanteans," "Lemurians" and other "lost" races belong squarely in the realm of the metaphysical, as their existence has been suggested by esoterics. This view is espoused by Argentine occultist and author Guillermo Terrera, who recounts the hidden lore surrounding the city of Erks, beneath the Andes, in his book "El Valle de los Espíritus." We are given the entire history of this magical metropolis, which boasts ownership of "the three sacred mirrors," through which the high priests and ascended masters of Erks can contact other subterranean cities and saucer-riding aliens from space. Terrera even provides us the names of the leaders of the High Council of Erks and those of the masters of the "Primordial School." Despite the Blavatskyesque implications, many scholars believe in Erks and have placed its location somewhere at the root of Mt. Uritorco in Argentina's Mendoza province.

Terrera goes on to say that the mechanical noises that can be heard at night in the vicinity of Mts. Uritorco and Pajarito, and which appear to emanate from below the ground, are the sounds being picked up by the "sacred mirrors," which act as radio telescope dishes. These sounds have allegedly been captured on audio tape: one is similar to an air hammer, another closely resembles that of a large set of gears being moved, and still another has been compared to the droning of a piece of factory equipment. Erks obtains light and free energy from "nuclear explosions produced by the liquid mass or magma at the earth's core." All knowledge concerning Erks has allegedly been gleaned through clairvoyants, psychometrists and parasensitives.

But Erks is far from being the only mystery Argentina has to offer. In the early 1970s, a missionary reportedly established a settlement with a few families in the locality of El Rosario in the Province of La Rioja. One of the settlers sought shelter in a cave during the rainy season and was startled to find a flight of stone steps leading into the mountain. Upon reaching the bottom of the stairs, the settler was astonished by a sight worthy of an Edgar Rice Burroughs novel: a city of gleaming buildings stood before his eyes, surmounted by domes and avenues paved by "what looked like acrylic." The architectural wonders weren't the only noteworthy feature, as the witness also saw the denizens of this underground paradise, describing them as "men clad in black tunics, while the women wore white." Illumination came from luminous orbs suspended in the air.

The settler returned to the surface and promptly informed the missionary in charge of the settlement - and the community's medical officer - of what he had found. All three men returned to the site, confirming the existence of the Shangri-La in the Andean Precordilleran region.

The discovery was subsequently made known to the Provincial Government of La Rioja, which dispatched its own forces to ascertain the veracity of the claim. Upon reaching the mountain, alas, they found "an impenetrable wall of stone." Researchers from Argentina's CATENT initiative were able to specify an exact date for the incident - September 23, 1970 - but little more.

OUR HOLLOW EARTH

"Niels Klim's journey under the ground being a narrative of his wonderful descent to the subterranean lands; together with an account of the sensible animals and trees inhabiting the planet Nazar and the firmament."
Baron Ludvig Holberg

JOURNEY UNDER THE GROUND

INTRODUCTION.

Ludvig Holberg, the author of the Narrative of Niels Klim, was the most eminent writer among the Danes in the eighteenth century. His works show a surprising versatility of genius, comprising Histories and Treatises on Jurisprudence, together with Satires and Comedies. He was by birth a Norwegian, but was educated at the University at Copenhagen in Denmark. Soon after receiving a theological degree from that Institution, he visited Holland and England, and resided about two years at Oxford.

Shortly after his return he published an "Introduction to European History," and an "Appendix to the Universal History," in which he gives an account of contemporaneous affairs in the principal governments of the world. His historical labors were interrupted by a royal appointment to a professorship in the University. This office he enjoyed for five years, and then went abroad. In his Autobiography he has given an interesting account of his travels, both at this time and subsequently, and has described men and manners in a way highly entertaining, and generally just. He visited most of the cities of Southern Europe, abiding some time in each. He was well received by men of letters, and made many valuable acquaintance, wherever he went. After remaining one whole winter at Rome, and accomplishing the object of his mission, he returned to Copenhagen. His income was now small, and for two years he was oppressed with great pecuniary difficulties. It was during this period that he published in the Danish language, his "Introduction to the Law of Nature and of Nations."

In this treatise, Holberg aimed rather to apply the principles of Natural Law to the Laws and Constitutions of Norway and Denmark, than elaborately to discuss the principles themselves. The work was coldly received at its first appearance, but, after ten or twelve years began to excite public attention, and passed through several editions.

At length, the professorship of metaphysics becoming vacant, he received the appointment. The emoluments of this office, though small, supplied his necessities, and, not long after, on obtaining a more lucrative station in the University, he was relieved from his embarrassments.

Hitherto, he had devoted himself almost exclusively to Jurisprudence, History and Languages, and had never tried his hand at poetical composition. Indeed, he had ever felt a strange aversion to the study of poetry, and, although he had read the Latin Poets, and composed Latin Poems, it was more for the sake of proficiency in the language, than for pleasure, or, in his own words, "as a sick man swallows bitter draughts, not because they are grateful to the palate, but, because they are recommended by the physicians."

He now, however, seemed inspired by a new ambition, and set himself to imitate one of Juvenal's Satires. Encouraged by his unexpected facility, he projected and composed an original poem. Its success, when published, surpassed that of any work previously written in the Danish language. Judicious critics heartily commended it, and some even looked upon it as introducing a new era in the national literature. It was also published in Sweden and Germany, and raised the author's reputation abroad. He next published five more Satires, prefixing to each a short preface, unfolding the writer's design. His poetical productions were a source of more honor than gain, and, becoming weary of almost profitless pursuits, he abandoned poetry, and devoted himself to his former studies.

Nevertheless, the solicitations of friends prevailed upon him to turn his attention to Dramatic composition. Here he was equally successful. His comedies were received with great applause, and still hold possession of the stage. Like his Satires, they were intended to expose fashionable vice and folly. They are twenty-five in number. The names of several will give some notion of their general character—The Babbling Barber; Always Busy and Doing Nothing; The Treacherous Step-father; The Political Tinman.

His health being impaired by unintermitted literary labor, he determined to seek relief from the baths of Aix-la-Chapelle. He did not derive from them the benefit he anticipated, but, after spending the winter in Paris, returned home with renewed health and spirits. His next publication, was a Satirical Poem, entitled "Metamorphosis," in which brutes and trees are transformed into men. This was the last of his poetical efforts.

For several years he had been engaged in preparing "A General Ecclesiastical History from the origin of Christianity to the Reformation of Luther," which he

OUR HOLLOW EARTH

now published. This production, the author affirms, was written with perfect impartiality. He sometimes censured the Fathers, praised heretics, when they deserved it, and occasionally even commended the Popes. It was extremely popular, though all were not pleased with its liberal spirit. A Comparative Biography of Asiatic and Indian Heroes, after Plutarch's style; A short Historical Account of his Native Town; The Narrative of Niels Klim; His Autobiography; and a History of the Jewish Nation, digested from the works of Josephus, Prideaux, and Basnage, close the list of his works.

"The Journey to the World under ground," or "Narrative of Niels Klim," had been written for a long time, but he had refrained from printing it from an unwillingness to provoke enmity. But the importunity of friends, and the generous offer of a bookseller finally prevailed, and he put it into the printer's hands. The following account of this performance is abridged from his autobiography.

There are many persons of both sexes in my country, who believe in fairies and supernatural beings, and who are ready to swear, that they have been conveyed by spirits to hills and mountain caves. This superstition is ridiculed in Klim, the hero of the tale. He is supposed to be transported to the world under ground, where he meets with some surprising adventures. Many strange creatures inhabit this new world; trees, for instance, are introduced, endowed with speech, and musical instruments discuss questions of philosophy and finance. Amongst the characters, those geniuses, who perceive everything at a glance, but penetrate nothing, are conspicuous.

People of quick perception, whom we use to admire, are despised by the Potuans, who look upon them as idle loungers, that, though always moving, make no progress. Prudent men, on the contrary, who measure their own strength, and advance cautiously, are greatly esteemed by that nation, though with us they pass for fools or cowards. The Potuans and Martinians are examples of both these extremes. By the former Klim was considered a blockhead, on account of the quickness of his perceptions; by the latter he was equally despised for the slowness of his apprehension.

To Klim, who measures virtues and vices by the ordinary standard, everything is a paradox; but what he at first condemns, he admires and extols after deliberation; so that the object of the whole work is to correct popular errors, and to distinguish the semblance of virtue and vice from the reality. Its subordinate design is to expose the monstrous fictions, which some authors obtrude upon us in their descriptions of remote countries.

"The Narrative of Niels Klim," though written so many years ago, contains many satirical hits, exceedingly applicable to the present time; thus showing that what appears to one age to be a whim altogether new, may be, in fact, only some old notion newly promulgated. Greater liberties were allowed at that period in literature than would now be permitted. Holberg's humorous productions are not wholly free from a fault, whose existence the taste of any age may explain, but does not excuse.

After living in competency for many years in Copenhagen, he was, in 1747, created a baron by the king of Denmark. He died in 1754.

APOLOGETIC PREFACE.

Since it has come to our ears that some persons have doubted the truth of this story, and that, consequently, the publisher of the subterranean voyage has gotten, here and there, a bad reputation, we have, to prevent all false accusations, held it advisable to prefix to this new edition certificates from men whose honesty and sincerity are raised above all distrust, and whose evidence will secure the publisher against all opposition. The first two of these witnesses we know to have been contemporary with our hero; the rest flourished at a period immediately subsequent; and all are generally known as people venerable in virtue and honesty, whose cool and sound judgments effectually preclude the blandishments of cajolery, while their noble candor and undeviating uprightness forbid the sanction of their names to whatever is, in its nature, deceitful or fictitious. With the testimony of such respectable persons, we shall bind the tongues of all false, prejudiced and sneering critics, and, before these signatures, oblige them to acknowledge their folly and take back their heedless accusations. The certificate sent to my brother and myself reads thus:

"At the desire of the estimable and much respected young men, PETER KLIM and ANDREAS KLIM, we, the undersigned, do certify, that among the books and papers left by the celebrated NIELS KLIM, we have seen a manuscript, with the title, 'Subterranean Voyage.' To the same 'Voyage' were added a subterranean Grammar and Dictionary, in two languages, namely, Danish and Quamitic. By comparing the celebrated Abelin's Latin translation with this old manuscript, we find that the former does not, in the least point, deviate from the hand-text. To its further confirmation we have hereby placed our seals.

ADRIAN PETERSON, MPP. JENS THORLAKSEN, MPP. SVEND KLAK, MPP. JOKUM BRANDER, MPP. JENS GAD, (for self and brother,) MPP. HIERONYMOUS GIBS, (Scotch,) MPP."

We hope by such distinguished and authentic testimony to remove all doubt; but should there be found any stubborn enough to persist in their suspicions, in spite of these certificates, we will anticipate their objections, and endeavor to subdue their incredulity with other weapons.

It is a known fact, that in a section of Norway, called Finnmark, exist people who have advanced so far in the study and practice of natural witchcraft, (a science into which other nations have scarcely looked,) that they can excite and subdue storms; transform themselves to wolves; speak several, and in our world en-

OUR HOLLOW EARTH

tirely unknown, languages; and travel from the north to the south pole in less time than one hour. One of these Finns, by name Peyvis, came lately to Bergen, and exhibited so many strange proofs of his art and science, that all present deemed him worthy of a doctor's hat: at the same time a fierce critic came out with a review of the "Subterranean Travels," which he assumptively tagged to the long list of "old women's stories;" the honor of the Klims being thus impugned, and his own by implication, Peyvis, through our influence, obtained permission to collect materials and prepare himself for a voyage under ground. He commenced by publishing a card, wherein he exalted his abilities in the following expressions:

What will you? say! From northern ice to southern land: From eastern isles to western sand, Spirits of earth, spirits of air; Spirits foul and spirits fair, My power obey! I break the rainbow's arched line; That herald of approaching calm. Thunder I send by cold moonshine,— Mine is the bane and mine the balm. My beck upwhirls the hurricane: The sun and moon and stars in vain Their wonted course would keep; Honey from out the rock doth weep When I command. My potent wand, Stretched on the mighty northern wave, Or seas that farther India lave, Subdues their mountain billows hoarse, To inland brooklets' murmuring course. What is on earth, what is in sea, In air and fire, from Peyvis free?

Everybody shuddered from fear at hearing these incredible assumptions. The Finn immediately prepared himself for the voyage, undressed, and, strange sight! suddenly transformed to an eagle, raised himself into the air and soon vanished. After a full month's absence, our wonderful doctor, early on a morning, re-appeared, entirely exhausted, his forehead streaming with sweat. When sufficiently recovered from his fatigue, he commenced a description of his adventures on his air passage and in the subterranean lands. He told us that on his arrival below, war was raging between the established government and the opposition, in which the party of Klim got the ascendancy, and reinstated the son of our Niels on the throne; our kinsman had for a long time borne the sceptre, under the administration of his mother; but now, old and glorified for many great feats, reigned alone over the whole subterranean world, with the name of Niels the Second.

Now, take shame to yourselves, ye incredulous mortals! and learn hereafter, in important matters, to proceed with more caution. Be ashamed, ye scoffers! and ask pardon for your unfounded accusations, your atrocious sneers. Stand abashed, finally, ye hyper-critics! and know that the learned world shall no longer suffer from your audacious and unreasonable judgments; then silence your stunted progeny at their birth, or if you will, yourselves!

OUR HOLLOW EARTH

CHAPTER I.
THE AUTHOR'S DESCENT
TO THE ABYSS.

In the year 1664, after graduating at the Academy of Copenhagen, in Theology and Philosophy, I prepared to return to my father-land, and took passage in a ship bound for the city of Bergen, in Norway. I had been furnished with brilliant testimonials from both faculties, and wanted only money;—a fate common to Norwegian students, who generally return home with empty purses from the Temple of the Muses.

We had a good wind, and in three days arrived at my native town, Bergen.

I occupied myself now, in expanding my knowledge of natural philosophy, and for practice, geologically examined the neighboring mountains. On the top of the most interesting of these mountains, (interesting I mean to a student,) was a remarkable cave, which the inhabitants of the town called Florien. From its mouth, a mild and not unpleasant air issues at certain periods, as though the cave inhaled the breeze and gently sighed it forth again.

The learned in Bergen, especially the celebrated Abelin and Edward, had longed to examine it; but these latter, from their great age, being unable to perform so arduous a feat, used every occasion to induce the young and adventurous to attempt the exploration. Instigated, (and it was a foolish, and I might say, a wicked resolution,) instigated, I say, not less by the encouragement of these great men than by my own inclination, I determined to descend into the cave. The longer I thought of the matter, the firmer I became. I prepared every thing needful for the expedition, and on a Thursday, at the morning twilight, departed from the city. I started thus early, because I desired to finish my labors before dark, and make a report the same evening.

How little did I then dream that like another Phaton, I should be driven head-

76

OUR HOLLOW EARTH

long through the air and precipitated to another globe, there to ramble for the space of ten years, before I should see my friends and native land again. The expedition took place in the year 1665. Accompanied by four men to carry the necessary implements, and assist in letting me down, I ascended the mountain. Arrived at the top, near the fatal cave, we sat down to breakfast. Now, for the first time, my heart began to faint, as though it foreboded my coming misfortune; but, in a moment, my half extinguished courage blazed again. I fixed a rope around my body, stood on the edge of the cave, and commended my soul to God.

Ordering the men to veer the rope steadily, and to hold when I cried out, I took a boat-hook in my right hand, and glided into the abyss. Aided by the pole, I was enabled to keep clear of the jutting points of rock that would have impeded my progress, as well as have wounded me. I was somewhat anxious about the rope, for it rubbed hard against the rocks at the top; and, in fact, I had scarcely descended twenty to thirty feet, when it gave way, and I tumbled with strange quickness down the abyss, armed like Pluto, with a boat-hook, however, in place of a sceptre.

Enveloped by thick darkness, I had been falling about a quarter of an hour, when I observed a faint light, and soon after a clear and bright-shining heaven. I thought, in my agitation, that some counter current of air had blown me back to earth. The sun, moon and stars, appeared so much smaller here than to people on the surface, that I was at a loss with regard to my where-a-bout.

I concluded that I must have died, and that my spirit was now about to be carried to the blessed dwellings. I immediately conceived the folly of this conclusion, however, when I found myself armed with a boat-hook, and dragging behind me a long strip of rope; well knowing that neither of these were needful to land me in Paradise, and that the celestial citizens would scarcely approve of these accessories, with which I appeared, in the manner of the giants of old, likely to attack heaven and eject the gods therefrom.

Finally, a new light glimmered in my brain. I must have got into the subterranean firmament. This conclusion decided the opinion of those, who insist that the earth is hollow, and that within its shell there is another, lesser world, with corresponding suns, planets, stars, &c., to be well-grounded. The result proved that I guessed right.

The rapidity of my descent, continually augmented for a long time, now began to decrease gradually. I was approaching a planet which I had from the first seen directly before me. By degrees it grew larger and larger, when, penetrating the thick atmosphere which surrounded it, I plainly saw seas, mountains and dales on its surface.

As the bold bird, between the billow's top And mountain's summit, sweeps around The muscle-clothed rock, and with light wing Sports on the foam, my body hovered.

I found now that I did not hang in the atmosphere, buoyed up by the strong current of which I have spoken, but that the perpendicular line of my descent was changed to a circle. I will not deny that my hair rose up on my head in fear. I knew not but that I might be metamorphosed to a planet or to a satellite; to be turned around in an eternal whirl. Yet my courage returned, as I became somewhat accustomed to the motion. The wind was gentle and refreshing. I was but little hungry or thirsty; but recollecting there was a small cake in my pocket, I took it out and tasted it. The first mouthful, however, was disagreeable, and I threw it from me. The cake not only remained in the air, but to my great astonishment, began to circle about me. I obtained at this time a knowledge of the true law of motion, which is, that all bodies, when well balanced, must move in a circle.

I remained in the orbit in which I was at first thrown three days. As I continually moved about the planet nearest to me, I could easily distinguish between night and day; for I could see the subterranean sun ascend and descend—the night, however, did not bring with it darkness as it does with us. I observed, that on the descent of the sun, the whole heavens became illuminated with a peculiar and very bright light. This, I ascribed to the reflection of the sun from the internal arch of the earth.

But just as I began to fancy myself in the near presence of the immortal gods, about to become myself a new heavenly light and wondered at as a brilliant star— behold! a horrible, winged monster appeared, who seemed to threaten me with instant destruction. When I saw this object in the distance I supposed it to be one of the celestial signs, but when it came near I perceived it to be an enormous eagle, which followed in my wake as if about to pounce upon me. I observed that this creature noticed me particularly, but could not determine whether as a friend or enemy.

Had I reflected, I should not have wondered that a human being, swinging round in the air, with a boat-hook in his hand, and a long rope dragging behind him, like a tail, should attract the attention of even a brute creature.

My uncommon figure gave, as I afterwards understood, occasion for strange reports to the inhabitants on my side of the planet.

The astronomers regarded me as a comet, with a very long tail. The superstitious thought my appearance to be significant of some coming misfortune. Some draughtsmen took my figure, as far as they could descry it, so that when I landed I found paintings of myself, and engravings taken from them, and hawked about.

But to return; the eagle flew towards me and attacked me with his wings very furiously. I defended myself as well as I could with my boat-hook, and even vigorously, considering my unstable situation. At last, when he attempted to grapple with me, I thrust the hook in between his wings so firmly that I could not extricate it.

The wounded monster fell, with a terrible cry, to the globe beneath; and holding the hook, I, well tired of my pendant attitude, was dragged to the planet.

At first my descent was violent, but the increasing thickness of the atmosphere as I approached the planet, made me sink with an easy and soft fall to the earth. Immediately on touching it the eagle died of its wounds.

It was now night; or rather the sun was down, for it was not dark. I could see clearly to read the papers I had in my pocket.

The light, as I have already said, comes from the firmament or internal shell of our earth, half of it being brightened at one time like our moon. The only difference between night and day is that the absence of the sun makes the weather a little colder.

CHAPTER II.
THE AUTHOR'S ARRIVAL AT THE PLANET NAZAR.

My voyage through the air was now ended. I lay for a long time entirely immovable, awaiting my fate with the approach of day. I now observed that the wants and weaknesses of humanity, which, during my passage had ceased, now returned. I was both sleepy and hungry. Fatigued in mind and body I fell into a deep slumber. I had slept, as far as I could judge, about two hours, when a terrible roar, which had previously disturbed my slumbers, suddenly waked me. I had dreamed some curious dreams; in one, I thought myself to be in Norway, at the church in my native town, listening to the singing of our clerk, whose voice was really unpleasant from its roughness. My first impression therefore, on recovering myself was, that this man was indulging in an extraordinarily ambitious strain. In fact, on opening my eyes, I saw a huge bull within a few feet of me. At the same moment, a vigorous roar from this animal convinced me that I did not listen to church music.

It was now day-break, and the rising sun began to gild the green oaks and fruitful fields, which, spreading abroad in every direction, astonished my recovered sense.

How much greater was my surprise when I saw the trees, of which there were great numbers in my view, move, although not a breeze stirred.

The vicinity of the bull not being pleasing to me, I arose and began to ascend a tree which stood near. As I raised myself by its limbs, it gave a low, yet shrill scream, and I got at the same time a lively slap on my ear, which propelled me headlong to the ground. Here I lay as if struck by lightning, about to give up my spirit, when I heard around me a murmuring noise, such as is heard on the Exchange when the merchants are assembled.

I opened my eyes and saw many trees moving about the field. Imagine my agitation, when one of the trees swept towards me, bent one of its branches, and, lifting me from the ground, carried me off, in spite of my woful cries, followed by an innumerable number of its companions of all kinds and sizes. From their trunks issued certain articulated sounds, which were entirely incomprehensible to me, and of which I retained only the words: Pikel-Emi, on account of their being often repeated. I will here say, these words mean an extraordinary monkey, which creature they took me to be, from my shape and dress. All this, of course, I learned after being some months among them.

In my present condition, I was far from being able to conceive of the nature of sensible, speaking trees. In truth, so confounded was I, that I forgot I could speak myself. As little could I understand the meaning of the slow, solemn procession, and the confused murmurs which resounded in the air.

I fancied they were reproaching or expressing their contempt of me. I was not far from the truth: for the tree into which I had climbed to escape from the bull, was no less than the wife of the sheriff of the neighboring town, to which they were now taking me a prisoner.

The buildings and streets of this town were very handsome and extensive. The houses, from their height, appeared like huge towers. The streets were wide and filled with trees, which swayed about and saluted each other by lowering their branches.

The greater this declination, the more expressive was it of respect and esteem.

As we passed through a very wide street I saw a tall oak approach a distinguished house, when the trees which escorted me, stepped gracefully back, and bent their branches to the ground. I concluded this must be a more than common personage. In fact, it was the sheriff himself, the very dignitary, whose lady it was insisted I had come too near. I was carried to the hall of this officer's house, and the door was locked upon me. Several trees armed with axes kept guard over me. The axes were held in the branches, which served the same purpose as human hands. I noticed that high up in the branches each wore a head, about the size of my own, covered with leaves and tendrils instead of hair. Below were two roots or legs, very short.

These trees were much smaller than those on our earth, in fact being about the height of a man; some indeed were much shorter; but these I concluded to be children.

While reflecting on the miserable situation in which I found myself, and weeping over the ill-luck of my adventure, my guards stepped up to me and commanded me to follow them. They led me to a splendid building in the middle of the market-place.

At the door of this building stood Justice, cut out in the form of a tree, holding among the branches a pair of scales. I presumed the structure to be the courthouse, nor was I deceived. I was carried into a large room, the floor of which was overlaid with glittering marble flags of various colors.

At the upper end a golden chair was raised a little above the floor, like a judge's seat; in it was seated a sedate palm tree, distinguished from the rest by the gorgeousness of his leaves; a little below him were seated twelve assessors, six on either side. About them stood twenty-four officers holding axes. I was not a little terrified when brought a prisoner before these magnates.

As I entered the hall, all the officers of the court stood up, elevated their branches and then sat down. After this ceremony I was placed at the bar between two trees, the stems of which were covered with sheep-skins. These persons I supposed to be lawyers, and so they were.

Before the trial commenced, the head of the judge was wrapped up in a black blanket. The accuser then made a short speech, which he thrice repeated. The lawyer appointed to defend me, replied in the same manner. A perfect silence then ensued. In half an hour the superior judge rose from the chair, removed the blanket, raised the branches towards Heaven, and spoke with much grace, what I supposed to be my sentence. I was then carried back to my prison.

While I mused on the strange things I had witnessed, a tree came into my cell, with an instrument resembling a lancet in his hand. He stripped one of my arms, and made a puncture in the median vein. When he had taken from me as much blood as he deemed sufficient, he bound up the wound with great dexterity. He then examined my blood with much attention, and departed silently, with an expression of wonder.

This circumstance by no means weakened the opinion which I had for some time entertained, that these people were shallow and foolish. But my judgment proved to be too hasty. When I was better enabled to judge of what passed about me, by acquaintance with the subterranean languages, my contempt was changed to admiration.

I will now explain the ceremonies, which to my ignorance seemed ridiculous.

From my figure it was concluded that I was an inhabitant of the firmament. I was supposed to have attempted to violate the person of a chaste and virtuous lady, and for this crime I had been taken to the court-house for trial.

The rising of the branches towards Heaven, was a common ceremony of religion. The lawyers were clothed in sheep-skin, to remind them of the attributes of their calling—innocence, faithfulness, and sedateness. The repetition of their speeches was on account of the very slow apprehension and cautious decision of the people, by which peculiarities they were distinguished from all the inhabitants of the subterranean world. But what most excited my curiosity was the history of the supreme judge. This was a virgin, a native of the town, and appointed by the King to the office of Kaki, or judge, for her superior virtue and talent. It must be observed that this nation pay no regard to sex in appointments to office, but, after a strict examination, elect those to take charge of affairs who are proved to be the most worthy.

OUR HOLLOW EARTH

Seminaries are established throughout the country, to teach the aspirants to public honors the duties appertaining to the direction of government. The business of the administrators of these colleges is to search closely into the brains and hearts of the young students, and when satisfied with their virtue and ability, to give to the king a list of those fully prepared to fill the public offices. The administrators are called Karatti.

The young virgin of whom I have spoken, had received, four years before from the Karatti, a certificate for remarkable attainments and virtues, and had been invested with the "blanket." This blanket was wrapped about her head during my trial; this precaution, however, is taken only in trials such as mine, in which the occasionally broad nature of the testimony might have a painful effect upon the virgin judge, should her face be exposed to the public gaze.

The name of this virgin was Palmka. She had officiated for three years with the greatest honor, and was considered the most learned tree in the city.

She solved with so much discretion the knottiest questions, that her decisions had come to be regarded as oracles.

As Themis' self, with scales of equal weight, She judged with candor both the small and great: The sands of truth she, like the goddess, frees From falsehood's glitter and from error's lees.

The following account was given to me of the blood-letting to which I had been subjected. When any one is proved to be guilty of a crime, he is bled, for the purpose of detecting from the color of the fluid, or blood, how far his guilt was voluntary or otherwise; whether he had sinned through malice or distemper. Should the fluid be found discolored, he is sent to the hospital to be cured; thus this process is rather a correction than a punishment. A member of the council, or any one high in office, would be removed, should it be found necessary to bleed him.

The reason why the surgeon, who performed the operation on me, was astonished, was, on account of the redness of my blood. The inhabitants having a sort of white fluid in their veins, the purity of which is proportional to their innocence and excellence.

I was put at my ease when I observed that the trees generally possessed a large share of humanity. This was displayed in their little attentions to me. Food was brought to me twice a day. It consisted of fruit and several kinds of beans; my drink was a clear, sweet and exceedingly delicious juice.

The sheriff, in whose house I was imprisoned, had immediately given notice to the King that he had by accident got possession of a somewhat sensible animal of an uncommon figure. The description of my person excited the king's curiosity. Orders were given to the sheriff, that I should be taught the language of the country; on which I should be sent to court. A teacher was appointed for me, whose instruction enabled me in a half year to speak very comprehensibly. After this preparatory course of private study, I was sent to the seminary, where particular care was taken both of my mental and physical education. Indeed, so enthusiastic were they to naturalize me, that they actually fastened branches to my body to make me look as much as possible like themselves.

CHAPTER III.
DESCRIPTION OF THE TOWN KEBA.

During the course of my education, my landlord frequently carried me about the town, and pointed out the most remarkable things. Keba is the town next in size and importance to the capital of the kingdom of Potu. The inhabitants are distinguished for their sedateness and moderation; old age is more respected by them than by any other community. They are strangely addicted to the pitting of animals against each other; or, as they call it, "play fight." I wondered that so moral a people could enjoy these brutal sports. My landlord noticed my surprise, and said, that throughout the kingdom it was the custom to vary their lives with a due mixture of earnest duties and amusing pleasures. Theatrical plays are very much in vogue with them. I was vexed, however, to hear that disputations are reckoned suitable for the stage, while with us they are confined to the universities.

At certain times in the year, disputants are set against each other, as we pit dogs and game cocks. High bets are made in favor of one or the other, and a premium is given to the winner.

Beside these disputants, who are called Masbakki, or boxers, various quadrupeds, wild as well as tame, are trained to fight as on our globe.

In this town a gymnasium is established, in which the liberal arts are taught with much success.

My landlord carried me, on a high festival day, to this academy. On this occasion a Madic, or teacher in philosophy, was elected. The candidate made a very prosy speech on some philosophical question, after which, without farther ceremony, he was entered, by the administrators, on the list of the public teachers.

On our way home from the academy, we met a criminal, led by three watchmen. By sentence of the kaki, he had been bled, and was now on his way to the city hospital. I inquired concerning his crime, and was answered, that he had publicly lectured on the being and qualities of God—a subject entirely forbidden in this country. Disputants on these matters are regarded as insane, and are always sent to the mad-house, where they are doctored, until they recover their sound reason. I exclaimed: Heaven and Earth! how would such laws operate on our globe, where thousands of priests quarrel every day about the divine attributes, the nature of spirits, and other secrets of the same character? Truly, here they would all be sent straight-way to the mad-house. These, among many other singular customs, I observed during my college life. Finally, the time came when, furnished with appropriate testimonies from the teachers, I was ordered to court. Here is my certificate. How angry and confused, was I, when I read it:—

"In accordance with your royal order, we hereby send the animal, which sometime since came down to us from the firmament; which animal calls itself man. We have, with sedulous care and patient industry, taught this singular creature in our school, and after a very severe examination, pronounce it to be very quick in its perceptions and very docile in its manners. Nevertheless, from its obtuse and miserable judgment—which we believe arises from its too hasty inferences—its ridiculous scepticism on unquestionable points, and its no less ridiculous credulity on doubtful ones, we may scarcely number it among sensible beings. However, as it is far quicker on its legs than any of our race, we humbly suggest, that it is very well adapted for the situation of a running-camp-footman. Written at our Seminary at Keba by your Highness' most humble servants.

NEHEK, JOKTAN, RAPASI, KILAK."

I returned sorrowfully to my landlord, and begged of him with tears in my eyes, to use his influence to alter the nature of my certificate from the Karatti, and to show them my testimony from the academy of Copenhagen, in which I was represented as a remarkable student. He replied to me, "that this diploma might be well enough in Copenhagen, where probably the shadow was regarded more than the substance: the bark more than the sap; but here, where the kernel was more important than aught else, it was of no use."

He counselled me to bear my fate with patience, and assured me, in the politest manner, of his friendship. Having nothing more to say, I made ready, without delay, for the journey. There travelled in company with me several small trees, which had been educated with me in the seminary, and were now destined to the capital for preferment.

Our leader was an old Karatti, who rode on an ox, because from his age he could not walk. Our progress was very slow, so that three days were occupied in our passage. We had a quick and comfortable jaunt, if I except the meeting with some wild monkeys, that would spring towards me, and pester me now and then. They evidently supposed me to be one of their race. I could not suppress my anger, however, when I observed that the trees seemed to perceive this mistake of the monkeys, which gave the saplings food for laughter at my expense. I must remark that I was carried to court in the same dress which I wore on my descent to the planet, with the boat-hook in my hand and the rope dragging after me. This was by order of the king, who wished to see me in my own bark.

CHAPTER IV.
THE ROYAL COURT OF POTU.

At last, we entered the large and splendid capital of the kingdom of Potu.

We were first carried to a house, where all students from the country seminaries are received, for the purpose of refreshment. Here we prepared for an interview with the king. In the mean time our Karatti, or leader went before to announce us to the court. On his return, we were all ordered to follow him. On our way to court we met several small trees, with printed stories in their branches. These were literary hawkers. I accidentally fixed my eye upon the title of one of these books. It was: "A true account of an entirely new and wonderful meteor, or flying dragon, which was seen last year in the heavens." I knew this was myself, and therefore purchased the book, for which three kilak—about two cents—were demanded. On the title page I found an engraving of myself, as I appeared while hovering over the planet, accompanied by boat-hook and rope. We now approached the castle, an extensive series of battlements and buildings, more distinguished for its strength and delicacy of finish than for splendor. It presented to my view a very singular, and, I may say rural, appearance, from the vast number of trees on the walls.

It was now noon, and the dinner hour. The king wishing to see me before he dined, I was brought alone to the dining hall. The king received me very graciously, uniting in a remarkable degree, while addressing me, mildness of tone with dignity of expression.

At my entrance into the hall, I knelt before the throne: the king demanded the meaning of the ceremony. Having told him the reason, he remarked, that such worship was due only to the Divinity. When I had raised myself, he put to me several questions—demanding how I had come down?—the reason of my journey—my name—where I came from, &c., all which questions I answered truly. Finally, he inquired concerning my religion, and was evidently much pleased with our creed. I was ordered to wait till dinner was over. At the table were seated with the King, the Queen, Prince, and Kadok, or great chancellor. At a certain sign, a maiden tree entered, bearing in her eight branches, as many dishes, which was the number daily served at the royal table. Another tree entered with eight bottles, filled with as many different juices. In the dinner conversation, frequent mention was made of myself.

After dinner, the King ordered me to show my testimony. After reading it, he looked at my legs. "The Karatti are perfectly right!" said he; "and their advice shall be followed." A Kiva, or secretary, was now sent for, to enter me, among others, in the royal register of promotion. This Kiva was a tree of remarkable external appearance; he had eleven branches—a singular number—and was able to write eleven letters at once. With this tree I afterwards became very intimate; he wrote all the letters which I, as footman, carried about the country.

On receiving my appointment, I went to bed. Although I was much fatigued, I could not get any sleep for a long while. However, I fell, at last, into an uneasy slumber, from which I was suddenly roused by an uncommonly large monkey, which, on opening my eyes, I found playing all manner of tricks with me, much to the amusement of several young trees, my companions. The king laughed heartily over the jokes of the monkeys, when they were related to him, but at the same time, ordered me to be clothed in the subterranean manner; that is, ornamented with branches, as I had been at my first arrival below ground. My European clothes were taken from me and hung up in the museum, with the following description attached:

DRESS OF THE CREATURES ABOVE GROUND.

After my fright from the monkey, I got no more sleep. In the morning I rose with the sun, and went to receive my charge for the day. An innumerable number of errands were given me to perform, together with letters and documents directed to all parts of the country.

This life I led four years; during my rambles I studied the character of the inhabitants, and copied, as far as possible, their habits. The people generally are distinguished for the politeness of their manners, and the sensibleness of their notions. The citizens of the town of Maholki, only, are wanting in refinement and judgment; they are thorn trees; very obstinate and crabbed in disposition, and great gossips, withal; let one take you by the button and you cannot get away easily.

Each province is peopled by its own race of trees; in the country each village has one sect; but the large cities contain a mixed population.

I had a good opportunity, as courier-general, to observe the peculiarities of these people, and I shall now describe their polity and religion, their laws and sciences.

OUR HOLLOW EARTH

CHAPTER V.

THE KINGDOM OF POTU AND ITS INHABITANTS.

The kingdom of Potu is enclosed within very narrow boundaries, and occupies but a small space of the inner globe.

The whole planet Nazar is scarcely six hundred miles in circumference, and may be travelled over its whole extent without guide or interpreter, for there is but one language throughout. As the Europeans on our globe take the first rank among the nations, so are the Potuans distinguished among the nations of Nazar for their virtue and understanding.

The roads are dotted by stone pillars, which, covered with inscriptions, denote every mile; affixed to them are hands pointing the road to every city and village;—splendid cities and prosperous villages! The country is intersected by greater and lesser canals, on which boats propelled by oars, skim with wonderful celerity. The oars are driven by self-moving machines, so quietly that very little motion is given to the water. The planet Nazar has the same motion with the earth, and all the peculiarities of the latter planet: night and day; spring, summer, autumn, and winter. The inhabitants consist of oak, lime, poplar, thorn, and pine trees, from which the months—there being six in each subterranean year—take their names.

The chronology is peculiar, being fixed by remarkable occurrences. Their oldest tradition is, that three thousand years ago, a mighty comet appeared, immediately after which followed a flood, which swept off all the races of trees, animals, &c., with the exception of one or two of each race, who saved themselves upon a high mountain, and from whom descended the present inhabitants. Corn and other grain with the fruits common to Europe, grow here in great profusion. The waters are filled with fish, and upon the banks of the rivers are seated splendid country houses. Their drink is prepared from certain herbs, which bloom at all times of the year.

In Potu is established a very useful law called the "generation law."

This law varies the liberties and advantages of the people according to the number of children each one possesses. Thus, he who is the father of six children is exempted from all common and extraordinary taxes. Therefore generation is quite as useful and desirable in this country as on the earth it is burthensome and dangerous: below ground never was such a thing imagined as a small-pox-tax.

No one can hold two offices at once. It is thought that each office, however small, requires the sole attention of its occupant, and that none should be employed in that which they do not understand.

I remember to have heard the philosopher Rakbasi speak thus: "Every one should know his own talents, and should impartially judge of his own merits and faults; otherwise the actor must be considered more sensible than natural men; for he chooses, not the best part, but that which he can execute best. Shall we allow the actor to be wiser on the stage than we in life?"

The inhabitants of this kingdom are not divided into classes; those alone being regarded who are noted for virtue and industry. The highest rank, if rank it may be called, is given to those who possess the greatest number of branches, they being enabled to do the most work.

Incola Terræ Musicæ.

OUR HOLLOW EARTH

CHAPTER VI.
THE RELIGION OF THE POTUANS.

The system of religion in Potu is very simple.

It is forbidden, under pain of banishment to the firmament, to explain the holy books; whoever dares to dispute the being and nature of the Deity, is sent to the mad-house and is bled. It is foolish, they say, to attempt to describe that to which our senses are as blind as the eyes of the owl in sunshine. All agree in worshiping a superior being, whose omnipotence has created and whose providence maintains all things. Each one is permitted to think and worship as he pleases; they only who publicly attack the prevailing religion, are punished as peace-disturbers. The people pray seldom, but with so ardent a devotion, that a looker-on would think them enraptured during the continuance of the prayer.

I told them that it was our custom to pray and sing psalms, while at our domestic duties. This they blamed. "An earthly king," said they, "would be angry should one who came to petition for something, brush his clothes and comb his hair in the presence of his sovereign."

They have many curious notions of religion, which they defend very artfully; for example, when I remarked to some of them whose friendship I had gained, that they could not expect to be blessed after death, since they walked in darkness here, they answered: "He, who with severity condemned others, was himself in danger of being condemned."

I once advised them to pray every day. They did not deny the importance of prayer, but thought true religion consisted in obeying the will of God. "Suppose," continued they, "that a king has two kinds of subjects: some err every day, violating from ignorance or malice the ruler's commands; they come each day with petitions and deprecations to the palace, beg pardon for their faults, and depart only to recommit them.

"The others come seldom, and never voluntarily to court, but execute faithfully and diligently every of the king's commands, and thereby evince the respect and loyalty due to him.

"Will not the king think these deserving of his love, as good subjects and faithful; but, on the contrary, those as evil subjects, burthensome as well for their misdeeds as for their frequent petitions?"

There are five festival days during the year. The first of these, which takes place at the beginning of the oak month, is solemnized with great devotion, in dark places, where not a ray of light is suffered to enter, signifying that the being they worship is inconceivable. The festival is called the "inconceivable-God's-day." The whole day, from sunrise to sunset, the people remain immovable, engaged in earnest and heart-felt prayer. In the four other festivals, thanks to God for his blessings form the principal ceremonies.

CHAPTER VII.

THE POTUAN CONSTITUTION.

In the kingdom of Potu the crown is inherited, as with us, by the eldest son of the king, whose power is absolute. The government, however, is rather fatherly than tyrannical. Justice is not meted and bounded by law alone, but is the result of principle, a principle of the widest philosophic comprehension. Thus, monarchy and liberty are closely united, which otherwise would be inimical to each other. The ruler seeks to maintain, as far as possible, an equality among his subjects. Honors are not limited to any class; but the poorer and more ignorant are called upon to receive their opinions from and submit to the decisions of the richer and more intelligent: the young are to respect the aged.

The annals of Potu show that some centuries ago, certain classes were highly favored by the laws to the exclusion of the great body of the people; frequent disturbances had been the result of this favoritism, till a citizen of the town Keba, proposed an alteration in the laws, by which all distinctions of class were abolished, and while the office of king should still remain hereditary, all the other officers of government should be subject to the will of the people, all of whom should be allowed to vote, who could read and write, at least, their names.

According to the custom of the subterraneans in such affairs, this intelligent and patriotic citizen was led to the market-place, with a rope about his neck: his proposition was considered, and after grave deliberation was adopted, as conducive to the general interest.

The mover was then carried in triumph through the city, honored by the grateful shouts of the people.

He, who has the most numerous offspring, is regarded as the most deserving citizen; he is honored above all others, without exception.

Such men are looked upon as heroes, and their memory is sainted by posterity. They only receive the name, which on the earth is awarded to the disturbers and enemies of the race—the name of—great!

It is very easy to conceive of the degree in which Alexander and Julius Csar would be prized by this people; both of whom not only had no children themselves, but murdered millions of the offspring of others.

I remember to have read the following inscription on the tomb of a Keban peasant:

OUR HOLLOW EARTH

"Here lies Jorktan the great, the hero of his time, father of thirty children."

Among the court officers the Kadori, or grand-chamberlain, is the superior. Next after him comes the Smizian, or treasurer. In my time, the seven-branched widow, Kahagna, filled the latter place. She was a virtuous and industrious woman; although her duties were many and important, she nursed her child herself. I remarked once, that I thought this to be troublesome and unfit for so great a lady. I was replied to in this wise: "For what purpose has nature given breasts to woman? for the ornament of the body alone,—or for the nourishment of their children?"

The crown prince was a child of six years; his governor was the wisest tree in the kingdom. I have seen an abstract of moral philosophy and policy, written by him for the use of the prince, the title of which is Mahalda Libal Helit, which in the subterranean language means, The Country's Rudder. It contains many fundamental and useful precepts, of which I recollect the following:

"1st. Neither praise nor blame should be too hastily credited; judgment should be deferred until accurate knowledge of the matter is obtained.

"2d. When a tree is accused of any crime, and the accusation is supported, then the life of the culprit must be examined, his good and evil actions must be compared, and judgment be given according to the preponderance of either.

"3d. The king must be accurately acquainted with the opinions of his subjects, and must strive to keep union among them.

"4th. Punishment is not less necessary than reward. The former restrains evil; the latter promotes good.

"5th. Sound reason teaches that especial regard should be had to the fitness of candidates to public offices; but, though piety and honesty go to form the greatest merit, yet, as the appearance of these virtues is often imposed on us for the reality, no tree should be severely judged till he gets into office, when he will show himself what he is.

"6th. To make a treasurer of a poor man, or a bankrupt, is to make a hungry wolf purveyor of the kitchen. The case of a rich miser is still stronger; the bankrupt or the penniless may set bounds to their peculation; the miser never has enough.

"7th. When the prevalence of vice renders a reformation necessary, great care and deliberation must be used; to banish at once, and in a mass, old and rooted faults, would be like prescribing laxative and restringent medicines at the same time to an invalid.

"8th. They who boldly promise everything, and take upon themselves many duties, are either fools who know not their own powers or the importance of affairs, or are mean and unjust citizens who regard their own and not their country's welfare."

CHAPTER VIII.
THE ACADEMIES OF POTU.

In this kingdom are three academies; one in Potu, one in Keba, and one in Nahami.

The sciences taught in them are history, political economy, mathematics, and jurisprudence. Their theological creed is so short that it can be written on two pages. It contains this doctrine simply, that God, the creator of all things, shall be loved and honored; and that He will, in an other life, reward us for our virtues and punish us for our vices. Theology forms no part of an academical course, as it is forbidden by law to discuss these matters. Neither is medicine numbered among the studies; for, as the trees live moderately, there is no such thing as internal disease.

The students are employed in solving complicated and difficult questions, and he who most elegantly and clearly explains his question, is entitled to a reward. No one studies more than one science, and thus each gets a full knowledge of his peculiar subject.

The teachers themselves are obliged to give, each year, a proof of their learning. The teachers of philosophy are required to solve some problem in morals; the historians, to elaborate some passage in history; the jurists, to elucidate some intricate point of law; these last are the only professors expected to be good orators. I told them that the study of rhetoric was common to all students in our colleges, and that all studies were merged in it. They disapproved of this, saying, that should all mechanics strive to make a masterly shoe, the work of most would be bad, and the shoemakers alone would win the prize.

Besides these academies, there are preparatory gymnasiums, where great pains are taken to discover the bent of the young, that they may be brought up in that science to which they are best fitted. While I was at the seminary of Keba, the bishop had four sons there, preparing for a military course; four others, whose father was a counsellor, were learning mechanical arts, and two maidens were studying navigation. The rank and sex of the scholars are entirely overlooked, in their regard to fitness and propriety.

OUR HOLLOW EARTH

He who challenges another to fight, loses forever his right to use weapons, and is condemned to live under guardianship, as one who cannot curb his passions or temper his judgment. I observed that the names of parties who go to law, are kept secret from the judge, he not being an inhabitant of the place where the trial is carried on. The object of this singular law is to prevent all partiality and bribery on the part of the judge, by withholding from him all knowledge of the influence or property of the litigants.

Justice is executed without regard to persons. The king, indeed, is not required to appear in court, but after death, his memory is put to the bar of public opinion, and his life is vindicated or condemned through the peoples' advocates. This trial takes place before the Senate, and judgment is freely pronounced according to the weight of the evidence. A herald proclaims the decision, which is inscribed on the king's monument. The words used in these trials are: Praiseworthy,—good,—not bad,—moderate,—tolerable. Sentence must be pronounced by one of these words.

The Potuans give the following reason for this custom. The living king cannot be brought to justice without causing rebellion. As long as he lives, the people owe to him blind obedience and constant reverence. But when the king is dead, the bond between them is dissolved, and, his memory belonging to them, they are bound to justify it as his virtues and vices principally affected themselves.

The Potuanic annals show that for centuries only one king has received the last degree of judgment—tolerable—or, in their tongue: Rip-fac-si. This was King Mikleta. Although the Potuans are well versed in arms, and defend themselves bravely, when attacked, they never make war on others.

But this king excited by a miserable desire to extend the borders of his empire, entered into an offensive war with his neighbors, and subdued many of them.

The Potuans gained, indeed, in power and wealth, but they suffered more from the loss of friendship and the increase of fear and envy in the conquered. The honorable regard for justice and equity, to which they had hitherto owed their prosperity and supremacy, began from that time to fade. On the death of Mikleta, however, the people recovered from their folly, and showed their regret for it, while at the same time they regained the good will of their neighbors, by putting a blot upon the memory of their ruler.

But, to return to myself. I took but little pleasure in associating with my companions, a set of absurd trees, who constantly ridiculed me for my quick perception.

This quality, I have already said, I was blamed for, very early in my career but by learned trees, with grave and dignified complaisance. These saplings, on the contrary, pestered me with silly nicknames. For example, they took a malicious delight in calling me Skabba, which means an untimely or unripe thing.

OUR HOLLOW EARTH

CHAPTER IX.

THE JOURNEY AROUND THE PLANET NAZAR.

I had now performed the toilsome duties of a courier for two years, having been every where with orders and letters. I was tired of this troublesome and unbecoming business. I sent to the king petition after petition, asking for my discharge, and soliciting for a more honorable appointment. But I was repeatedly refused, for his majesty did not think my abilities would warrant promotion. He condescended to refer me to the laws and customs, which allowed those only to be placed in respectable and important offices, who were fitted for them by talent and virtue. It was necessary, he continued, that I should remain where I was, till I could, by my merits, pave my way to distinction. He concluded thus:

Study to know yourself, is wisdom's rule; The wise man reasons,—blunders, still, the fool. Strive not with feeble powers great weights to move, Before your shoulders long experience prove.

I was thus obliged to remain, as patiently as I could, in my old service, amusing myself in thinking how to bring my talents to the light. In my continual journeys about the country, I studied the nature of the people, the quality of the soil; and, in short, became accurately acquainted with every thing worthy of observation. That I might not forget any thing, I used myself to write notes of each journey. These notes I enlarged afterwards, as well as I could, and was thus enabled to deliver to the king a volume of considerable size.

I soon observed that this work was far from being displeasing to his majesty. He read it through with attention, and then recommended it to the senate with much ceremony. It was soon determined that I should be made use of to discover and make known whatever there was of interest throughout the planet. Truly! I expected some other reward for my sleepless nights and laborious days, than still greater burthens, still heavier travail. But I could only in silence sigh with the poet:

"Alas! that Virtue should be praised by all,— Should warm, with its mild beams, all hearts: Yet mock and freeze its owner."

However, as I have always had a great desire to see and hear every thing new,

OUR HOLLOW EARTH

and expected, withal, a magnificent reward from the really kind-hearted king on my return, I set about this work with a kind of pleasure.

Although the planet Nazar is but about six hundred miles in circumference, it seems, to the trees, of vast extent, principally on account of their slow movement. No Potuan could go round it in less time than two years, whereas, I, with my long legs, could traverse it easily in two months.

I set out on this journey in the Poplar month.

Most of the things which I shall now relate, are so curious, that the reader may be easily brought to believe them to be written from mere whim, or at least to be poetical contrivance. The physical and moral diversities are so many and so great, on this planet, that a man who has only considered the difference between the antipodal nations of the earth, can form but a faint idea of the same. It must be observed that the nations of Nazar are divided by sounds and seas, and that this globe is a kind of Archipelago.

It would be wearisome to relate all my adventures, and I shall limit my remarks to those people who seemed to me the most remarkable.

The only things which I found in common with all, were figure and language. All were trees. But in customs, gestures, and sense, so great was the diversity, that each province appeared like a new world.

In Quamso, the province next to Potu, the inhabitants are entirely oak trees. They know not of bodily weakness or disease, but arrive in perfect and continued health to a very great age. They seem to be the most fortunate of all creatures; but I found, after some intercourse with them, that this assumption was a great mistake. Although I never saw any of them sad, yet none appeared to be happy. The purest heaven is never impressive, but after a storm; so happiness is not appreciated by these oaks, because it is never interrupted; they bless not health, because they are never sick. They spend their lives in tame and uninterrupted indifference. Possessed of little politeness and goodness of heart, their conversation is cold and cheerless; their manners stiff and haughty. Without passions, they are crimeless; without weakness, they are pitiless.

Those alone to whom pain and sickness bring the remembrance of their mortality, learn in their own sufferings, to sympathise with and compassionate the woes of others.

I was now in a land, where I had a living proof of how much the occurrence of pain and the fear of death tend to produce mutual love and cheerful converse among fellow beings. Here, for the first time, I came to know the folly and sin of grumbling at the Creator, for bringing upon us trouble and suffering, which are really good for us, and which produce the happiest consequences.

The province Lalak, which is sometimes called Maskatta, or the Blessed Land, was the next in the order of my journey. This land is very appropriately named.

OUR HOLLOW EARTH

All things spring forth spontaneously:

> Here, between melon vines and moist strawberry, Flow milky brooks and amber streams of mead; There, luscious wine, from crystal, spouts more merry, As Bacchus from his slumber had been freed. Far down along the mountain's verdant side, The limpid juice, with golden lustre, ripples. In dales, soft undulating, oozing glide Sweet waters, out of teeming nature's nipples; And trees of Paradise their branches reach, Bending with purple plum and mellow peach. From all the land nutritious savors rise, To bless its sons, then mount to scent the skies.

These advantages do not, by any means, make the inhabitants happy. It occurred to me, that laborers in harsher climates are much better off than these people, who necessarily languish in idleness and luxury.

Next to Lalak is Mardak, inhabited by cypresses. Of these are different descents or races, determined by the number or shape of their eyes. Here is a list of the varieties:

Nagiri, who have oblong eyes; to whom all objects appear oblong.

Naquire, whose eyes are square.

Palampi, who have very small eyes.

Jaraku, with two eyes, which are turned in opposite directions.

Mehanki, with three eyes.

Panasuki, with four eyes.

Harramba, whose eyes occupy the whole forehead; and finally,

Skodolki, who have a single eye in the neck.

The most numerous and powerful of these races, are the Nagirians. Kings, senators and priests are always chosen from this class. None are admitted to any office, but those who acknowledge and testify by oath, that a certain table, dedicated to the sun and placed in the temple, is oblong. This table is the holiest object of mardakanic worship. The oath, to be taken by aspirants to honors, is as follows:

"Kaki manaska quihampu miriac jakku, mesimbrii caphani crukkia, manaskar quebriac krusondora."

In English:

"I swear, that the holy table of the sun seems oblong to me, and I promise to remain in this opinion until my last breath."

When the neophyte, of either class, has sworn this oath, he is taken up among the Nagirians, and is qualified for any office. On the day after my arrival, as I walked in the market-place, I met a party bearing an old man to the whipping post. I asked them the nature of his offence, and was told that he was a heretic, who had publicly declared that the holy table of the sun appeared square to him.

I immediately entered the temple, being curious to know whether or not my eyes were orthodox. The table was certainly square to my view, and I said so to my landlord, on my return. This tree, who had been recently appointed a church-warden, drew a deep sigh on this occasion, and confessed that it also seemed square to him, but that he dared not express such an opinion, openly, from fear of being ejected from office, if not worse.

Trembling in every joint, I quietly left this region, fearful that my back might suffer on account of my heterodox vision.

The duchy of Kimal is considered the mightiest and richest of the states on this planet. There are numberless silver mines within its borders: the sand of its rivers is colored by gold, and its coasts are paved with pearl oysters of the finest water.

The people of this province, nevertheless, are more miserable than those of any other I visited. They are miners, gold-strainers and pearl-divers, condemned to the most infamous slavery, drenched in water, or secluded from air and light, and all for the sake of dear gain. How strange and senseless is the lust for brilliant baubles!

The possessors of wealth are obliged to keep a continual watch over their property, for the land is full of robbers. None can travel without an armed retinue. Thus, this people, on which their neighbors look with longing eyes, should deserve pity rather than excite envy. Fear, mistrust and jealousy rage in all hearts: each regards his neighbor as an enemy. Sorrows and terrors, sleepless nights, pale faces and trembling hands are the fruits of that very wealth, which their neighbors look upon as the greatest good.

My wanderings through Kimal were the most unpleasant and dangerous in all my experience. My course was towards the east. I journeyed among many people, who were generally polite and social, but whose customs were not singular enough to merit particular attention. I had much cause to wonder, when I came among the Quambojas, in whom nature was entirely perverted. The older these people grow, the more lustful they become. Rashness, lasciviousness and roguery increase with years. None are suffered to hold offices after the fortieth year. At this age, the wildness and moral insensibility of boyhood begins; the sports of childhood, only, are tolerated. The tree becomes a minor, and is placed under the guardianship of his younger relations.

I did not think it advisable to remain long in Quamboja, where in a few years, I should be sentenced to become a child again.

I witnessed a perversion of a different kind in Kokleku. In the former province, nature is the agent of this perversion; here the law is the agent. The Koklekuans are juniper trees.

The males alone cook and perform all domestic duties. In time of war, they serve in the army, but always in the ranks. To the females, are entrusted all civil, divine and military offices. The females reason thus: The males are endowed with greater bodily strength, and greater powers of endurance; therefore, it is clear that nature intended them to do all the work. But this will keep them so busy, that they will not have time to think. Moreover, as continual physical labor degrades the mind, if they should presume to think, their thoughts would be puerile, and practically useless. Therefore, it is plain, that to the females belongs the direction of affairs. The lady of the house may be found in the study with books and papers about her, while the master is in the kitchen cooking and washing.

I saw many mournful effects of this inconsistent custom.

In other places, females are to be found, who bring their chastity to market and trade with their charms. Here the young males sell their nights, and for this end congregate in certain dwellings, before which signs are hung out. When these males get to be too troublesome, they are punished as prostitutes are, elsewhere. Females stroll about the streets, beckon to the men, stare at them, whistle and cry psh! to them; chuckle them under the chin and do all manner of tricks, without the least sense of shame. These females boast of their victories, as dandies, with us, plume themselves on their intimacy with ladies, whose only favor may have been a sharp box on the ear. None are here blamed for besieging a young male with love letters and presents. But a young fellow would be looked upon as having outraged all decency, should he stammer out a faint yes, to the first entreaty of a young female.

At the time I was in the country a terrible commotion arose on account of the violation of a senator's son by a young virgin. She was generally condemned for this high-handed and abominable action. The friends of the youth insisted that she should be prosecuted, and if the crime were proved, sentenced to mend the young fellow's honor by marrying him, especially as it could be sworn to that he had lived a pure and virtuous life till this libertiness had seduced him.

Blessed Europe! I exclaimed on this occasion; thrice blessed France and England! where the names—weaker sex—frail vessels—are no idle names:—where the wives are so entirely subjected to their husbands that they seem to be rather machines or automatons than creatures endowed with free will and noble aspirations!

The most splendid building in Kokleku is the Queen's harem, in which three hundred beautiful young fellows are shut up for life. So jealous is the queen, that no female is allowed to approach the walls within one hundred yards. Never beholding any of their race but the queen and a few dried-up and ugly spinsters, the poor creatures vegetate, mindless and joyless.

Having heard, accidentally, that my form had been praised in the presence of the queen, I hastily escaped from this unnatural and execrable land:

—Fear to my feet gave wings.

Continuing my course still to the east, I came to the philosophical-land, as its inhabitants, who are principally engaged in the study of philosophy and the sciences, vain-gloriously call it. I had long and earnestly wished to see this land, which I enthusiastically ascribed to be the seat of the muses.

I hurried on with all possible celerity. But the roads were so full of stones, holes and bogs, that I was delayed, besmirched, and bruised. However, I endured these troubles patiently, anticipating the delights that awaited me, and well knowing that the path to paradise is not over roses. When I had struggled onward for an hour I met a peasant, of whom, after saluting him, I demanded how far distant the borders of Maskattia were? "You should rather ask," he replied, "how far you must go back;—for you are now in the very middle of it!"

In great astonishment I asked, "How is it, that a land inhabited by pure philosophers, should appear like the abode of wild animals and ignorant barbarians?" "Indeed," said the peasant, "It would look better if the people could find time to attend to such trifles. At present they must be excused, for they have higher and nobler things in their heads: they are now speculating about the shortest road to the sun. Nobody can blow and swallow at the same time."

I understood the meaning of the cunning peasant, and left him, after getting the direction to the capital city, Casea. Instead of guards and the usual collection about the gates of a large town, hens and geese strutted about at their ease: in the crevices of the gate hung birds-nests and cobwebs.

In the streets philosophers and swine were mingled together, and both classes being alike filthy, they were only to be distinguished from each other by form.

The philosophers wore a kind of cloak, of the color of which I should not dare to give an opinion, so thick was the dirt upon them. I was run into by one of these wise men, who seemed to be enraptured by some speculation.

"I beg pardon, master of arts!" I exclaimed, "may I ask of you the name of this town?" He stood for some time immovable, with closed eyes; then recovering somewhat from his trance, and rolling his eyes upwards, he muttered: "We are not far from noon!"

This untimely answer, which betrayed a perfect insensibility, convinced me that intelligence resulting from methodical and practical study is preferable to the torpid insanity incident to much learning.

I went on, hoping to meet with some sensible animal, or any body rather than a philosopher. In the market-place,—a very extensive square,—were a great many statues and pillars, covered with inscriptions.

I approached one of them to get, if possible, the meaning of the characters. While engaged in spelling the words, my back suddenly became warm, and immediately after I felt warm water trickling down my legs. I turned round to discover the fountain of the stream, and, lo! an abstracted philosopher was performing, at ease on my back, the same operation that the dogs do against the study.

OUR HOLLOW EARTH

This infamous trick excited my wrath, and I gave him a severe blow.

The philosopher regained his wits at this, and seizing me by the hair, dragged me around the market-place. Our struggles soon brought us both to the ground. Then a multitude of philosophers came running towards us, and having dragged me from under my opponent, beat me with their sticks till I became senseless. I was then carried to a large house and thrown into the middle of the hall. I now recovered in a measure from my ill treatment.

On seeing this, the wise man who first insulted me, recommenced to beat me, notwithstanding my prayers for mercy. I now learned that the intensity of no anger can be compared to the philosophical; and that the teachers of virtue and moderation are not called upon to practise the same. The longer my oppressor beat me, the more did his blood boil. At last there came into the hall four sophists, whose cloaks proclaimed them to be of a different class from my late tyrants. They had some compassion for me, and soothed the rage of the others. I was taken to another house, and right glad was I to escape the hands of the bandits, and get among honest people.

I related to my protectors the cause of the calamity. They laughed heartily at the whole matter, and then explained to me that the philosopher, absorbed in deep thought, had mistaken me for a pillar before which it is customary, on certain natural occasions, to stop.

Just when I supposed myself in safety. I nearly gave up the ghost from fear. I was led into a dissecting room, filled with bones and dead bodies, the stench from which was intolerable.

After languishing in this disgusting den for half an hour, the lady of the house brought in my dinner, which she had prepared herself. She was very polite and amiable; but looked at me closely, and sighed continually. I asked the reason of her sorrow. She answered, "that she became sick when she thought of what I was to suffer."

"You have, indeed," she said, "come among honest people, for my husband, who lives in this house, is a doctor of medicine, and the others are his colleagues: but your uncommon figure has awakened their curiosity, and they have determined to take your internal structure into close consideration. In fine, they intend to cut you up, in the hope of finding some new phenomena in anatomy." I was thunder-struck at hearing these tidings. I cried out indignantly:

"How can people be called honest, madam! who entertain strangers only to cut them up?"

"You should stick your fingers in the ground," she replied, "and smell the land you have got into!" I begged her with tears in my eyes to intercede for me. She answered, "My intercession would be of no service to you: but I will endeavor to save you by other means." She then took my hand, carefully led me out by a back door, and guided me to the city gate.

Here I would have taken leave of my kind and gentle guide; but while manifesting my gratitude in the most lively expressions, she suddenly interrupted my speech and signified her intention not to leave me till I should be in perfect safety. She would not be persuaded to return. We walked on together. Meanwhile she entertained me with just and sensible remarks on the customs and follies of the people. Afterwards she turned the discourse to more delicate matters. We were at some distance from the city. My soft companion adverted to the danger from which she had saved me, and suddenly demanded of me, in return, a politeness which was morally impossible.

She told me with much feeling and warmth of the unfortunate fate of females in this land:—that the philosophers, entirely absorbed by their speculations, and buried among their books, neglect to an alarming extent, the duties of marriage. "Yes," she continued, "I can swear to you, that we should be wholly undone if some polite traveller did not occasionally take pity on our miserable condition, and mitigate our torments."

I pretended not to understand her meaning, and showed the usual commonplace and complacent sympathy.

But my coolness was as oil to the flame. I increased my pace. The poor lady, whose heart had hitherto been subjected to the sweet-smiling goddess, now changed to a fury.

I fled from my new danger. Fear and length of legs enabled me to outstrip her. Mingled with her shrieks, opprobrious epithets fell fast; the last I could distinguish were: Kaki Spalaki:—ungrateful hound!

I passed on to other provinces, in which I found but little uncommon and peculiar.

I now thought that I had seen all the wonders of Nazar. But when I came to the land of Cabac, more curious and more incredible things were disclosed to my gaze. Among the Cabacans there is a certain class without heads. These are born without that appendage. They speak through a hole in the middle of the breast. On account of this natural defect, they are generally excluded from offices where brains are thought to be useful. They are notwithstanding a serviceable class: the most of them are to be seen at court; being gentlemen of the bed-chamber, stewards of the household, keepers of the harem, &c.

Beadles, vestry-clerks and such brainless officers are chosen from this class.

Occasionally one of them is taken up into the senate, either by the particular favor of government, or through the influence of friends. This is done, generally, without injury to the country; for it is well known that the business of the country is carried on by a few senators, and that the rest are only useful to fill the seats, and agree and subscribe to the determinations of the leaders.

OUR HOLLOW EARTH

The inhabitants of the two provinces, Cambara and Spelek, are all lime trees. But their resemblance ends in form. The Cambarans live only about four years. The Spelekians, on the other hand, attain to the wonderful age of four hundred years.

In the former place, the people have their full growth a few weeks after birth, and finish their education before the first year. During the three remaining years they prepare for death. The province appeared to be a true Platonic republic, in which all the virtues reached to their perfection. The inhabitants, on account of their short lives, are, as it were, continually on the wing. They regard this life as a gate through which they hastily pass. Their hearts are fixed on the future rather than on the present. They may be called true philosophers, for they care not for luxury and pleasure, but strive through fear of God, virtuous actions, and clear consciences, to make themselves worthy of eternal happiness. In a word, this land seemed to be the habitation of saints and angels;—the only school of virtue.

I was here brought to think of the unreasonableness of those who grumble at the shortness of life,—those quarrellers with providence! Life can be called short when passed in luxury and idleness. The shortest life is long when it is well employed.

In Spelek, on the contrary, all the vices common to erring creatures seem to be congregated. The people have only the present in their minds, for the future has no sensible vanishing point. Sincerity, honesty, chastity and decency have taken flight to give place to falsehood, lasciviousness, and bad manners.

I was happy to get away from this province, although I was obliged to traverse desolate and rocky regions which lay beyond it. These deserts separate Spelek from Spalank, or the "Innocent Land."

This name is obtained from the meekness and innocence of the inhabitants. These are all stone oaks, and are thought to be the happiest of all sensible beings. They are not subject to any agitation of mind, and are free from all vices.

Free, of compulsion ignorant, did all obey The simple rules of nature. Justice easy And virtue unadorned they practised; for unknown Were punishment and fear. On no holy stone Were menaces engraved: no holy table Declared the thunders of the law. None trembled At the ruler's frown or nod: but, without guard,— With sharpened steel on shoulder ready poised,— Or castled wall bristling with murder's tools, Were all ranks safe. On no battle-field Was victor crowned or bloody altar Heaped with his kinsmen's corpses. With sports And pleasant tales, in infant innocence they lived (The innocence that lies in mother's lap unstained.) Thus passed they from the fond embrace of peace, With easy change to Death's determined grasp.

When I came to this province, I found that the reputation which these people had gained, namely: that they practised virtue from inclination rather than from the authority of law—was well founded.

But as envy and ambition were entirely unknown to them,—the inducements to excel, and the will for great things were wanting.

They had no palaces, no courts, no fine buildings. They had no magistrates to administer law; no avarice to carry them to court. In fine, although without vices, they knew nothing of the arts,—of splendid virtues,—nor of any of the things which refine a people. They appeared to be rather an oak forest than a sensible and thoughtful nation.

I travelled next through the province Kiliak. The natives of this province are born with certain marks on their foreheads, which point out how long they will live. At first I imagined these people to be happy, as death could never overtake them unexpectedly, nor tear them away in the midst of their sins. But as each one knows on what day he shall die, it is usual to postpone repentance till the last hour. They only are really pious who begin to sing their death song.

I saw several move about the streets with drooping heads and miserable looks—the signs upon their foreheads proclaimed their speedy dissolution.

They counted their remaining hours and minutes upon their fingers, and regarded with horror the rapidity of time.

The Creator's wisdom and goodness to us in this respect became obvious to me in this land. I could no longer doubt that it is better for us to be ignorant of the future.

From Kiliak I sailed over a black sound to the kingdom of Askarak; there new wonders greeted me. While in Cabac, people are to be seen without heads, here, on the contrary, individuals come into the world with seven heads. These are great universal geniuses. In former times, they were worshiped with almost divine veneration, and were made senators, chief magistrates, &c. As they had as many plans and expedients as heads, they executed with zeal and rapidity many different things, and while the government was in their hands, there was nothing left unchanged.

But as they made several sets of ideas effective at once, it happened, very naturally, that these ideas came in contact with each other. At last, they mingled together so intricately, that the seven-headed geniuses could not discriminate in from out. The affairs of government became so disordered that centuries were required to restore them to the simplicity from which these all-knowing magistrates had brought them.

A law had been established, before I went there, by which all seven-headed people were excluded from important offices, and the administration of government was given to simple and ordinary persons, that is, persons with but one head.

The many-headed now occupy the same places as the headless of Cabac.

Beyond Askarak, and separated from it by extensive deserts, lays the Duchy of Bostanki. The Bostankins resemble the Potuans in their external form. Their internal construction is very singular. The heart is placed in the right leg; so that it may be literally said of them, that their hearts are in their breeches.

They are notorious for being the greatest cowards among all the inhabitants of Nazar.

Angry, from faintness and fatigue, I came to a tavern near the city gates. I could not abstain from growling at the landlord because he could not provide what I called for. The poor fellow fell on his knees before me, begged my pardon amid tears and groans, and held his right leg towards me that I might feel how his heart beat.

At this I laughed, and almost forgot to be angry. I wiped the tears from the poor sinner's eyes, and told him not to be afraid. He rose up, kissed my hand, and went out to prepare my food. Not long after, I heard lamentable cries and howls in the kitchen. I hastened thither, and to my great astonishment, saw the humble and trembling Monsieur poltroon engaged, very valiantly, in beating his wife and servant girls. When he perceived me he took to flight. I turned to the weeping wife and girls and demanded what could have excited such terrible anger in my lamb-like host. They stood for some time, silently, with their eyes fixed on the ground. At length, the wife replied in the following words: "You do not seem, dear stranger! to have much knowledge of human nature. The citizens of this place, who dare not look at an armed enemy, and, at the least noise, creep like mice into holes, hector in the kitchens, and tyrannize over us feeble women."

Thoroughly disgusted by the mean and cowardly spirit of this people, I hired a boat to go to Mikolak. On landing I missed my outer coat, which I recollected to have put in the boat at starting. After quarrelling a long time with the boatman, who denied all knowledge of it, I went to a magistrate, and related the whole matter to him. I asserted that I had at least a right to demand my own property, if I could not sue at law one with whom I had entrusted my goods.

The boatman still denied the theft, and required that I should be punished for wrongly accusing him. In this doubtful case, the court demanded witnesses. This demand I could not answer, but proposed that my opponent should take oath on his innocence.

At this proposal the judge smiled and said: "In this land, my friend, there is no weight in religious confirmation. The laws are our gods. Proof must, therefore, be given in a formal manner, by witnesses or written documents. Whoever cannot do this not only lose their case, but are subject to punishment for malicious accusation. Prove your case by witnesses, and you will get your own again." I lost my case, but from regard to the hospitality due to strangers, was not punished.

I had far more reason to pity this people than to regret my own loss. How weak is that society which relies for its safety on bare human laws. It is like a city built on a volcanic mountain! Little firmness has that political structure which rests not on the foundation of religion.

Leaving this atheistic land, I crossed a very high mountain to Bragmat, which lays in a dale at the foot of the mountain. The people of this city are juniper trees. The first that I met rushed towards me, and pressing with the weight of his body, felled me to the ground. When I demanded the reason of this rough salutation, he begged my pardon in the most polite and elegant expressions. A few minutes after, another struck me in the side with a hedge-pole, and likewise excused his carelessness in a pretty speech. I thought they must be blind, and gave to all I passed a very wide berth.

I was afterwards informed that some among them were possessed of a very sharp sight, so that they can behold objects far beyond the view of others, but they could not see what was directly before them. These sharp-sighted people are called Makkati, and are, most of them, adepts in astronomy and transcendental philosophy.

I passed through several other provinces, in which I found nothing worthy to be recorded in this history; and returned to Potu after an absence of two months.

I entered the city of Potu on the tenth day of the Ash month. The first thing I did was to deliver my journal to the king, who ordered it to be printed.

It must be observed that the art of printing, which both the Europeans and Chinese claim to have invented, has been well known in Nazar for ages. The Potuans were so much pleased with my book that they were never tired of reading it. Little trees carried it about the streets and cried: "Court-footman Skabba's Travels around the Globe."

Puffed up by my success, I now strove for higher things, and awaited, somewhat impatiently, an appointment to a great and respectable office. My expectations not being answered, I gave in a new petition, in which I eulogized my work and claimed a suitable reward for my uncommon merit.

The mild and beneficent king was moved by my prayers, and promised to keep me in gracious remembrance.

He kept his promise, but not to my liking, for his grace consisted only in making an addition to my stipend.

I had pointed my nose another way, but not daring to press the king with more petitions, I made my complaint to the great chancellor. This very sensible personage listened to me with his usual urbanity, and promised to serve me. At the same time he advised me to abandon my unreasonable desires, and take a more exact view of my weak judgment and general insignificance. "Nature," he said, "has been a step-mother to you; you want, altogether, the talents which clear the road to important offices. You must creep before you walk; and it is foolish to think of flying without wings." He acknowledged my merits: "But," he continued, "it is not such merits as yours that will give you admittance to State affairs. If all merit should give this right, then every painter and sculptor, this for his skill in carving, that for his knowledge of colors, might demand a seat at the council board. Merit ought to be rewarded, but the reward should be adapted to the object, that the State may not suffer."

This speech struck me, and had the effect to keep me very quiet for some time. But I could not endure the thought of growing grey in my base employment. I determined on the desperate attempt, which I had formerly considered, to improve the constitution, and thus, by a bold stroke, to advance my own and the country's welfare.

Shortly before my journey I had strictly examined the internal condition of the kingdom, to discover the least failing in its machinery, and the best means to remedy it.

In the province Kokleku I had learnt that the government waggles in which women have a part. For being by nature vain, they strive to extend their power in every conceivable direction, and stop not till they have procured for themselves perfect and unlimited dominion.

I concluded, therefore, to propose the exclusion of the fair sex from all public offices, and trusted to get a sufficiency of voices on my side by placing the case in its best light. It seemed an easy matter, to me, to convince the male sex of the dangers to which they were exposed, if they did not, in time, weaken this female power.

I executed this plan with all the art I was possessed of, supporting it with the most cogent reasons, and sent it to the king.

He, who had given me many proofs of his favor, was astonished at this miserable and impertinent project, as he graciously called it, and said, that it would fall out to my destruction.

But relying partly on my reasonings and partly on the support of the whole male population, I held obstinately to my plan. According to law, I was led to the market-place with a rope about my neck, to await the decision of the Council. When the counsellors had given their votes, the sentence was sent to be subscribed by the king, which being done, it was publicly read by a herald, as follows:

"On mature consideration we adjudge, that the proposal made by Sr: Skabba, first court-footman to his majesty, to exclude the second sex from public offices, cannot be accepted, without affecting the peace and order of the kingdom: since the women, who form the half of our population, would naturally be excited by this innovation, and thereby become hostile and troublesome to the government. Furthermore, we hold it to be unjust to deny, to trees of excellent qualities, admission to offices of which they have hitherto shown themselves to be worthy and especially it is incredible, that nature, which does nothing inconsiderately, should have idly endued them with superior and varied gifts. We believe the welfare of the kingdom requires that a regard should be had to fitness rather than to names, in the disposal of offices. As the land is not seldom in need of capable subjects, we pronounce a statute which should declare an entire half of the inhabitants, merely from birth, unworthy of and useless in affairs, to be deplorable.

"After grave deliberation we declare this to be justice: let the aforesaid Skabba, for his no less despicable than bold proposal, suffer the usual punishment in such cases."

The good king took my misfortune to heart, but did not seek to change the resolution of the Council. As a matter of form he signed the warrant for my execution. Yet with his characteristic mildness, and in consideration of my having been born and educated in a strange world, where a quick and reckless head is thought to be a blessing, he commuted my punishment to imprisonment till the beginning of the Birch month, when, with other animals, I should be banished to the firmament. When this sentence was published, I was sent to prison.

CHAPTER X.
THE VOYAGE TO THE FIRMAMENT.

Twice a year, some very large birds, called Kupakki or post birds, are wont to show themselves on the planet Nazar.

They come and go at certain regular periods, which has given rise to various opinions. Some think, that insects, of which great multitudes appear at the same periods, and which the birds are very fond of eating, entice them down to the planet. This is my own notion. The circumstance, that when these insects disappear, the birds return to the firmament, places the opinion almost beyond all doubt. It is the same instinct, which leads certain species of birds on our earth to migrate at regular periods.

Others believe, that these birds are trained like hawks and other birds of prey, to fetch booty from other lands. This conjecture is grounded upon the great care with which they lay down their burdens, when their flight is finished. This supposition is somewhat strengthened by the fact, that they become tame and gentle just before they begin their flight, suffering themselves to be thrown into nets, under which they lie immovable. Meanwhile they are fed with insects till the regular period arrives. Then a long box, just large enough to hold a tree or man, is fastened to a rope, which is again tied to the legs of the bird. On the banishment day, food is withheld from them, the nets are raised, and the kupakkis wing their way to the firmament.

Two citizens of Potu had been doomed to banishment with myself. One was a metaphysician, who had offended the law by making some sage remarks upon the nature of spirits; the other was a fanatic, who, by starting doubts concerning the holiness of religion and the uniting force of the civil law, was suspected to have designed the overthrow of both. This latter would not regulate himself by the public ordinances, because, he said, all civil obedience was inconsistent with his conscience. Thus three of us, namely, a project-maker, a metaphysician, and a fanatic, were, on the first day of the Birch month, shut up in boxes.

I never knew what became of my fellow-sufferers. As for myself, I was enclosed, with food sufficient for a few days. Shortly after, my kupakki, finding nothing to eat, started off with amazing speed.

It is generally believed, under ground, that the distance between the planet Nazar and the firmament is about four hundred miles. I had no means of determining how long my passage was, but conjectured it to be about twenty-four hours.

I heard nothing, during this time, but the heavy and monotonous flapping of the kupakki's wings. At last, there sounded in my ears a confounding noise, which announced that we could not be far from land.

I now observed that the bird had really been trained, for he set the box, with so much care on the ground, that I did not feel the slightest jar. The box was immediately opened, and I rose up in the midst of a great multitude of monkeys, who, to my astonishment, conversed together in an intelligent language rather than chattered, and walked to and fro, in measured and dignified paces. They were dressed in cloths of varied colors. A number of them advanced towards me with much politeness, and handed me from the box.

They seemed to be surprised at my figure, particularly when they discovered I had no tail. Their amazement was not at all lessened by the fact, that I resembled them (laying aside the tail) more nearly than did any stranger they had hitherto seen.

At the time of my arrival the water was very high, owing to the nearness of Nazar. This planet has the same effect upon the tides of the firmament, as our moon has upon those of the earth.

I was led to a very large building, ornamented in the richest style. The presence of a guard at the door convinced me that it was the residence of no common monkey. It was, as I afterwards learnt, the residence of the mayor of the monkeys.

A number of teachers were selected to instruct me in their language.

In three months I was enabled to speak with considerable readiness. Then I expected to procure for myself the admiration of all, for my prompt ingenuity and superior memory. But my teachers declared me to be sluggish and dull of apprehension, and in their impatience often threatened to abandon their charge. As, on the planet Nazar, I had been ironically named Skabba, or the untimely, for my quick perceptions, so here I was called Kakidoran, which signifies, idle and stupid. Those only are respected here, who can comprehend and express any thing instantaneously. I amused myself during the course of my studies by walking about the city, in which I met on all sides notable signs of splendor and luxury.

When I had finished my education, that is, when I could speak fluently, I was carried to the capital city Martinia, from which the whole country takes its name. The object of the mayor evidently was, to insinuate himself into the favor of a certain counsellor, by presenting to him a strange and unprecedented animal.

The government of Martinia is aristocratical. The state is administered by a great council, selected from the body of the old nobility.

OUR HOLLOW EARTH

Before proceeding to the house of the lord, to whom I was to be offered, the mayor led me to a hotel, where we could make ourselves presentable to his excellency. Several servants, called maskatti, or dressers, joined us for this purpose. One took the mayor's sword to burnish it; another tied different colored bands to his tail. I will here remark, that nothing lays nearer to a monkey's heart than the adornment of his tail.

When my conductor was polished, dressed and adorned, we departed for the president's palace, followed by three servants.

On coming to the entrance, the mayor loosed his shoes, that he might not soil the marble floor. After waiting for a long time, with not a little impatience, we were suffered to enter the reception hall. Here the president sat in a golden chair.

As soon as he saw us, the president burst out in a terrific laugh. I concluded either that he was seized by delirium, or that silly and insane laughter was a peculiarity of great people in Martinia. In short, I took his lordship to be a fool.

I afterwards expressed this opinion to the mayor; but he assured me that the president was a monkey of remarkable natural powers; that his mind was so comprehensive, that he not only determined matters of the highest importance at table, with his glass in hand, but even wrote or dictated a new statute between the courses.

His excellency tattled to me half an hour, his tongue wagging, the while, with an agility immeasurably superior to that of our European barbers.

Then turning to my companion, he said, he would take me among his subordinate attendants, since he perceived, from my sluggish disposition, that I must have been born in the land of stupidity, where

Long-eared mortals, in perpetual fogs, Oft lose their way to mire in horrid bogs:—

and consequently that I was unfit for any office of trust and respectability. "I have, indeed," urged the mayor, "observed a natural obtuseness in this man; nevertheless, when he is allowed time to think, he judges by no means badly."

"Of what use is that," replied the president; "here we need nimble officers, for the immense diversity of our affairs does not give us time to think."

The president, having spoken thus, very gravely, and carefully examined my body, and directed me to lift a heavy weight from the floor. Seeing that I did this with ease, he remarked: "Nature, although she has stinted you in the faculties of the soul, has compensated, in some measure, by granting to you a degree of bodily strength."

I now received orders to go out and wait in the court. Soon after the mayor followed, and as he passed, told me that his excellency had determined to include me in his train.

OUR HOLLOW EARTH

I concluded from his lordship's undervaluing opinion of me, that my situation could not be very elevated; still, I was curious to know my fate, and therefore asked the mayor if he knew what I was to be entrusted with. The mayor answered: "His excellency, with special grace, has appointed you for his chief porteur,[1] with a yearly pay of twenty-five stercolatus." (A stercolatu is about one dollar of our money.) "Furthermore, he will not require your services for any but himself and her grace, his lady." This answer was like a thunder-stroke to me; but I was sensible that it was useless to object.

I was carried to a chamber, where a supper of dried fruits was laid; after eating a little, my bed was pointed out to me.

I threw myself upon the bed, but my mind was so agitated, that I could not for a time close my eyes in sleep. The pride and contempt with which the monkeys regarded me, provoked me almost to rage. A more than Spartan patience was needed to listen with indifference to their sneers. At last I slumbered. How long I know not, for in the firmament there is no division of night and day. It is never dark, except at a certain period, when the planet Nazar comes between the firmament and the subterranean sun.

On awakening, I found at my side a mean looking monkey, who asserted that he was my colleague: He had brought with him a false tail, which he fixed upon me, and then tied to it some ribbons of various colors. He told me that in half an hour the president would be ready to set out for the Academy, and that I must prepare myself to begin my duties. The ceremony of promoting a doctor was to take place.

We bore the president to the Academy in a golden sedan, and were suffered to remain in the hall during the performance.

At the entrance of the president, all the doctors and masters of art rose and turned their tails towards him. To a dweller on the earth, such salutations would probably have appeared unseemly and ridiculous, as such a movement with us is expressive of indifference or dislike.

But every land has its own customs. I have seen so many strange ceremonies and varied usages, that I have come to observe, rather than laugh at them.

The act of promotion, on this occasion, was performed with the following ceremonies. The candidate was placed in the middle of the hall. Then three officers, each with a pail of cold water, approached him with measured steps. Each in turn dashed his bucket of water in the candidate's face. The sufferer is obliged to receive this bath without distorting his countenance, on pain of forfeiting his degree. Odorous oils were then sprinkled over him, and finally a powerful vomit was given to him. When this last dose had produced its usual effect upon the candidate, he was pronounced to be a lawfully graduated doctor.

I turned to a learned doctor, who stood near me, and humbly asked him the

OUR HOLLOW EARTH

meaning of all I had seen.

First expressing his pity for my ignorance, the sneering pedant condescended to inform me, that the ceremony of the water was significant of the preparation for a new course of life and duty; the ointment, of elevation above the mass; and the vomit, of the extermination of prejudice and error.

I fancied, but I did not say so, that my dignified instructor in the mysteries needed a fresh vomit.

The Martinianic religion is not at all practical. There are two hundred and thirty speculations concerning the form and being of God, and three hundred and ninety-six of the nature and qualities of the soul. There are many churches and theological seminaries, but in neither is taught the way to live and die well. The people are all critics, who go to be amused by the art and delicacy of the holy teachers. The more obscure and involved the propositions of their preachers, the more are they praised. The Martinians are indifferent to every thing they can easily understand.

Martinia is the paradise of project-makers. The more inconsistent and useless a scheme, the surer is it of general approbation.

When I once spoke with an enthusiastic monkey, of the earth and its inhabitants, he fell upon the notion, to bore through to the surface, and make a convenient and easy way of communication.

He prepared a long and eloquently worded plan on this subject, which pleased and excited every body.

A company was formed, and named the "Subterranean Boring Company" its originator, Hiho Pop-coq, was made its president. The stock was seized on with avidity, and the project was not abandoned until a multitude of families had been ruined, and the public affairs brought into the greatest disorder; and even then the scheme was dropped, less from its supposed impracticability, than from the length of time required to accomplish it.

The author of it was not only left unpunished, but was overwhelmed with the general applause, for the originality and boldness of his attempt.

The Martinians are used to console themselves on such occasions, by repeating the following couplet:

"The project ended in defeat; The notion was, however, neat."

When I had thoroughly studied the character of this people, I determined to take advantage of their weaknesses, and by some outrageous proposal, to gain their respect, and thereby better my condition.

I revealed my intention to a shrewd old monkey, who encouraged me in these words:

Who would succeed in Martinianic land, Must quit the useful, to propose the grand; Hazard those deeds, that to the gallows pave, Thy fortune's made! Here's honor for the knave.

After due deliberation, my choice became fixed upon that ornament for the head, called wigs by us.

I had previously noticed that the land contained a multitude of goats; with the hair of these creatures I proposed to manufacture my wigs.

My step-father had been engaged in the trade, and as I had, with the inquisitiveness of youth, observed the process, I could bungle at it.

I made a goat's-hair wig for myself, and adorned with it, presented myself to the president.

This dignitary was astonished at the new and uncommon decoration. He seized it from my head, and placing it on his own, hastened in a very undignified manner to the mirror.

So enraptured was he at the sight of the pompous protuberance, that he shrieked out: "Divine art, how like a God am I!"—he sent immediately for her Grace to partake in his joy.

She was not less pleased than her lord. She embraced him, kissed him, and assured him that she had never seen him more handsome.

The president addressed himself to me with much less haughtiness than usual. "O Kakidoran!" he exclaimed, "if this discovery of yours pleases the Council as well as it does me, your fortune is made. You may hope for the most honorable reward the State can give."

I gracefully thanked his Excellency, and immediately wrote a petition, which I requested him to lay before the Council.

His Excellency took the petition together with the wig, and departed. I understood that all the cases which were to come before the Council on this day, had been laid aside, so inquisitive were all to hear and examine my project. The work was accepted, and an appropriate reward was adjudged to me. I was called up to the council-chamber on my entrance, an old monkey stood up, and, after thanking me in the name of the whole republic, proclaimed that my work should be rewarded as its merits deserved. He then demanded, what length of time I should need to fabricate another such head ornament? I replied, that it was reward enough for me, that my curious workmanship had gained the approbation of the great men who composed the Council; for the rest, I bound myself to make another wig in two days, and also to manufacture wigs enough for the whole city in a month, provided I might count upon the assistance of a number of monkeys, accustomed to work. This proposal, however, made the president hot about the ears, and he exclaimed with much eagerness: "It is not fit, my dear Kakidoran, that this ornament should be common to the whole town, for being worn by all without distinction, it will become ordinary and vulgar. The nobility must necessarily be distinguished from the common people."

OUR HOLLOW EARTH

All the members of the Council concurred in his opinion, and the city marshal was charged to take heed that none might wear wigs, except the nobility. This order having been promulgated, the citizens thronged about the council-chamber to obtain titles and charters, which some bought with their money and others procured through the influence of their friends; so that in a short time full half the city were made nobles. But when petition after petition poured in from the provinces, that the like favor should be extended to them, the Council, being possessed with a righteous fear of riot and civil war, finally determined to allow every one, without distinction of rank, to wear a wig. I thus had the pleasure to see the whole Martinianic nation wigged before I left that country. And, truly, it can scarcely be imagined what a funny and ridiculous appearance the wigged monkeys presented! The whole nation made so much of my project and its accomplishment, that a new era was established; and from this time the wig-age commenced in the Martinianic annals.

In the meantime, I was loaded with praises and panegyrics, wrapped in a purple cloak, and returned from the court-house in the president's own sedan, the same porteur, who had formerly been my companion, serving me now as a horse. From that day I dined continually at the table of his Excellency.

With this glittering preamble to my fortunes, I commenced in earnest the work I had promised, and soon finished wigs enough for the whole Council; and after sweating for a month—a patent of nobility was brought to me, couched in the following words:

"In consideration of the most excellent and very useful discovery, through which Kakidoran, born in Europe, has made himself worthy of the gratitude of the whole Martinianic nation, we have resolved to advance him to the rank of nobility, so that he, and all his descendants shall be regarded as true noblemen, and enjoy all the prerogatives and rights, of which the nobility of Martinia are in possession. Furthermore, we have determined to dignify him with a new name; he shall therefore from this day, be no longer called Kakidoran, but Kikidorian. Moreover, since his new dignity requires a richer style of living, we grant him a yearly pension of two hundred patarer. Given in the council-chamber of Martinia, the fourth day of the month Merian, under the great seal of the Council."

Thus I suddenly became changed from a simple porteur to a respectable nobleman, and lived for a long while in great splendor and honor. When it was known that I was high in the favor of the president, everybody sought my good will and protection. It is the fashion among the poets of Martinia to panegyrize the tails of eminent monkeys, as it is with us to eulogize the beauty of women. Several poets commended the beauty of my tail, although I had none. To say everything on this subject in a few words—their fawning servility towards me was so extreme, that a certain man of high rank and station, did not hesitate, nor did he feel himself

OUR HOLLOW EARTH

shamed, to promise me that his wife should make herself agreeable to me in every possible way, provided that I would recompense him by recommending him to the president.

When I had lived in this land for the space of two years, at first a porteur and latterly a nobleman, an incident, entirely unexpected, occurred, which was nearly fatal to me. I had, up to this period, been in special favor with his Excellency; and her Grace, the president's lady, had evinced so much kindness to me, that I was regarded the first among all her favorites. She was distinguished for her virtue; but, when in the lapse of time, I perceived one after another ambiguity in her expressions, I began to feel a kind of mistrust, especially when I observed that

Sometimes she'd smile with wanton grace, Then unto sudden tears give place, While gazing, silent, on my face With mild devotion. Her's all the art of tenderness, That pleases while it wounds no less: Her breasts, half-covered, now confess Their strange emotion. Then sighs that can no reason find, Or used to make my reason blind:— Her hands upon her breast entwined— Ah, female charms! Her face would lose its rosy hue For lily's, washed in morning dew; Aurora's purple blazed anew, In love's alarms.

My suspicions finally became certainties, when a chambermaid brought to me, one day, the following note:

"DEAREST KIKIDORIAN,—

"The feeling which I owe to my rank and high descent, and the modesty natural to my sex, have until now hindered the sparks of love which have long secretly burned in my bosom, from breaking forth in open flame: but I am weary of the combat, and my heart can no longer resist its bewitching enemy. Have pity for a female, from whom only the utmost degree of burning love could have been able to extort a confession.

PTARNNSA."

I cannot describe how singularly I felt at this entirely unexpected declaration of love: but as I held it far better to expose myself to the revenge of a furious female, than to sin against the order of nature, by a shameful intimacy with a creature that did not belong to my race, I immediately wrote an answer in the following words:

"GRACIOUS LADY,—

"The constant favor his Excellency, your husband, has shown to me; the undeserved benefits he has bestowed upon me; the moral impossibility of fulfilling your gracious desires; and many other reasons, that I will not name, move me to submit to the anger of my gracious lady, rather than consent to an action that would stigmatize me as the most ungrateful and the lowest among all two-legged creatures. Besides, what is desired of me, would be more bitter to satisfy than death itself. This action, if I yielded to it, would effect the ruin and dishonor of one of the

OUR HOLLOW EARTH

most respected families in the State, and my willingness would injure, before all others, that person who has desired it. With the most solemn and sincere assurances of gratitude I must here declare, gracious lady, that under no circumstances can I fulfil your wishes in this respect, although to all other commands I promise a blind obedience.

KIKIDORIAN."

Underneath I wrote the following admonition:

"Think of this heavy sin; Fly ere it be too late: Shall vice, the pander, newly in, Bow virtue to the gate? Let Cupid not ensnare you— His cunning wiles beware you, The sweets of sin soon vanish— Its pains, ah! who can banish."

This letter I sent to the lady, and it had the effect that I expected; her love was changed to the bitterest hatred:—

In vain her glowing tongue would vie, To tell her frightful agony. Despairing shame her accents clip;— They freeze upon her snowy lip. No tears did flow; such pain oft dries The blessed current of the eyes: Fell vengeance from her black orbs glanced, While like a fury, she advanced.

Nevertheless, she restrained her fury, until she recovered the love-letter she had written to me. As soon as she had secured it, she hired some persons to testify by oath, that, in the absence of his Excellency, I had attempted to violate her. This fable was represented with so much art and speciousness, that the president did not doubt its truth, and I was ordered to be put in prison. In this, my despairing condition, I saw no other means of deliverance than to confess the crime, with which I had been charged, and supplicate the president for mercy: which being done, my life was conceded, but I was doomed to perpetual imprisonment. My charter of nobility was immediately taken from me, and I was sent to the galleys as a slave. My destination was to one of the ships belonging to the republic, which then lay ready to sail for Mezendares, or the Land-of-wonders. Thence were brought the wares that Martinia cannot produce. This ship, on board of which my evil fortune had now cast me, was propelled both by sails and oars; at each oar two slaves were chained: consequently I was attached to another unfortunate. I was consoled, however, by the prospect of a voyage, during which I hoped to find new food and nourishment for my insatiable inquisitiveness, although I did not believe all that the seamen told of the curious things I should see. Several interpreters accompanied us; these being made use of by the Mezendaric merchants in the course of their commercial negotiations.

OUR HOLLOW EARTH

CHAPTER XI.
THE VOYAGE TO THE LAND-OF-WONDERS.

Before I proceed to the description of this sea-voyage, I must first caution all severe and unmerciful critics not to frown too much at the narration of things, which seem to war against nature, and even surpass the faculties of faith in the most credulous man. I relate incredible but true things, that I have seen with my own eyes. Raw and ignorant ninnies who have never started a foot from their homes, regard every thing as fable, whose equal they have never heard of or seen; or, with which they have not been familiar from childhood. Learned people, on the contrary, especially those who have a deep knowledge of natural history, and whose experience has proved to them how fruitful nature is in changes, will pass a more reasonable sentence upon the uncommon things narrated.

In former days a people were found in Scythia, called Arimasps, who had but one eye, which was placed in the middle of the forehead: another people, under the same climate, had their foot-soles turned out backwards, and in Albany were people born with gray hairs. The ancient Sanromates ate only on every third day and fasted the other two; in Africa were certain families who could bewitch others by their talk; and it is a well known fact, that there were certain persons in Illyria, with two eye-balls to each eye, who killed people by merely looking at them: this, however, they could do, only when they were angry; then their fierce and scintillating stare was fatal to whomever was rash or unfortunate enough to meet it: on the mountains of Hindostan were to be found whole nations with dog's heads, who barked; and others who had eyes in their backs. Who would believe this and even more, if Pliny, one of the most earnest writers, had not solemnly assured us, that he had neither heard nor read the least hereof, but had seen it all with his own eyes? Yes, who would have imagined that this earth was hollow; that within its circumference were both a sun and moon, if my own experience had not discovered the secret? Who would have thought it possible, that there was a globe, inhabited by walking, sensible trees, if the same experience had not placed it be-

OUR HOLLOW EARTH

yond all doubt? Nevertheless, I will not pick a quarrel with any one, on account of his incredulity in this matter, because I must confess, that I myself, before I made this voyage, mistrusted whether these tales might not have arisen from the exaggerated representations of seamen, or that they were the result of that well-known qualification of this class of men, familiarly styled the "spinning a yarn."

In the beginning of the month Radir, we went on board our ship, weighed anchor, and

The wind in swelling sails embraced the bending masts,
And, like an arrow in the air, with lightning speed,
The keel shrieked through the foaming billows.

The wind was fair for some days, during which we poor rowers had a comfortable time, for the oars were not needed; but on the fourth day it fell calm;

The sails did fall: in haste the seats were fixed;
With plashing stroke, the oars smote heaven in the waters.

For a long time we met with nothing; but as soon as we lost sight of land, strange figures raised themselves from the quaking gulph. They were mermaids, who, when the weather becomes calm and the billows rest themselves, rise to the surface and swim towards any passing ship, to ask for alms. Their language was so similar to the Martinianic, that some of our sailors could speak with them without an interpreter. One of these singular creatures demanded of me a piece of meat; when I gave it to her, she looked at me steadily for a time, and said: you will soon become a hero, and rule over mighty nations! I laughed at this divination, for I considered it empty flattery, although the sailors swore to it, that the mermaids' prediction seldom failed. At the end of eight days we came in sight of land; which the seamen called Picardania. As we entered the harbor, a magpie came flying towards us, which, they said, was the custom-house inspector-general. When this dignitary had flown thrice around the ship, he returned to the shore and came back with three other magpies: these seated themselves on the prow of the ship. I came very near bursting with laughter, when I saw one of our interpreters approach these magpies, with many compliments, and heard him hold a long conversation with them. They had come for the purpose of examining our freight and detecting any forbidden articles that we might have concealed; when all was found correct, we were suffered to unload. As soon as this was done, a number of magpies flew to the ship, who proved to be merchants. The captain then went ashore, accompanied by myself and two monkeys, namely, our supercargo and an interpreter; after clearing the ship and disposing of the cargo, we returned, and shortly set sail.

In three days we reached Music-land. After casting anchor, we went on shore, preceded by one of the interpreters, who carried a bass-viol in his hand. As we found the whole country about us empty and desolate, discovering no where any trace of living creatures, the captain ordered a trumpet to be sounded, to inform the inhabitants of our arrival. Before the echoes of the blast from the trumpet had subsided, (and they seemed to penetrate farther and reverberate longer than usual from the perfect stillness of this apparently void region,) about thirty musical instruments came hopping towards us. These were bass-viols. On the very long neck of each was placed a little head; the body was also small, and covered by a smooth bark, which, however, did not close entirely around the frame, but was open in front and disposed loosely about them. Over the navel, nature had built a bridge, above which four strings were drawn. The whole machine rested on a single leg, so that their motion was a spring rather than a walk. Their activity was very great, and they jumped with much agility over the fields. In short, we should have taken them for musical instruments, as their general appearance purported, if they had not had each two arms and hands. In the one hand was a bow, the other was used upon the frets. When our interpreter would converse with them, he put his viol in its position, and commenced playing an air. They immediately answered him by touching their strings, and thus alternating with each other, a regular musical conversation was carried on. At first they played only Adagio, with much harmony; then they passed over to discordant tunes; and finally concluded with a very pleasant and lively Presto. As soon as our people heard this, they leaped and sung for joy, saying, that the bargain for the wares was now fixed. Afterwards I learnt that the Adagio, they first played, was merely an opening or preface to the conversation, and consisted only of compliments; that the discordant tones which followed, were bickerings and disputes about prices; and, finally, that the sweet sounding Presto indicated that an agreement had been made. At the conclusion of these negotiations, the wares stipulated for were landed. The most important of these is Kolofonium, with which the inhabitants rub their bows or organs of speech.

Late in the month of Cusan, we set sail from Music-land, and after some days sailing hove in sight of a new land, which, on account of the foul smell that reached our noses at a great distance, our seamen supposed to be Pyglossia.

The inhabitants of this land are not very unlike the human race in their general appearance; the sole difference being, that these people have no mouth: they speak from the face which turns towards the south when the nose points to the north. The first of them who came on board, was a rich merchant. He saluted us after the custom of his nation, by turning his back towards us, and immediately began to bargain with us for our wares. I kept myself considerably remote during the negotiation, as neither the sound nor the smell of his speech pleased me. To my great horror our barber was taken sick at this time, so that I was obliged to summon a Pyglossian perfume. As the barbers here are quite as talkative as among us, this one, while shaving me, filled the cabin with so disagreeable a smell, that, on his departure, we were obliged to smoke with all the incense we had on board.

OUR HOLLOW EARTH

We sailed hence to Iceland. This land consisted of desolate rocks, covered by eternal snows. The inhabitants who are all of ice, live here and there in the clefts of the rocks on the tops of the mountains, where the sun is never seen, enveloped by almost perpetual darkness and frost. The only light they have comes from the shining rime.

These lands, of which I here have given a view, are all subject to the great emperor of Mezendora proper, and are therefore called by seafaring people the Mezendoric islands. This great and wonderful country, namely, Mezendora, is the goal of all extended voyages. Eight days sail from Iceland brought us to the imperial residence. There we found all that realized, which our poets have fancied of the societies of animals, trees and plants; Mezendora being, so to speak, the common father-land of all sensible animals and plants. In this empire each animal and every tree can obtain citizenship, merely by submitting to the government and laws. One would suppose, that, on account of the mixture of so many different creatures, great confusion would prevail among them: but this is far from the case. On the contrary, this very difference produces the most happy effects; which must be attributed to their wise laws and institutions, decreeing to each subject that office and employment to which his nature and special faculties are best fitted. Thus, the lion, in consideration of his natural magnanimity, is always chosen regent. The elephant, on account of his keen judgment, is called to sit in the State-council. Courtiers are made of chameleons, because they are inconstant and know how to temporize. The army consists of bears, tigers and other valorous animals; in the marine service, on the contrary, are oxen and bulls; seamen being generally hardy and brave people; but severe, inflexible, and not particularly delicate in their living, which corresponds very well with their element. There is a seminary for this class, where calves or sea-cadets are educated for sea-officers. Trees, for their natural discretion and gravity, are usually appointed judges: counsellors are geese; and the lawyers of the courts in ordinary are magpies. Foxes are generally selected as ambassadors, consuls, commercial-agents, and secretaries-of-legation. The ravens are chosen for dealing-masters and executors on the effects of those deceased. The buck-goats are philosophers, and especially grammarians, partly for the sake of their horns, which they use on the slightest occasion, to gore their opponents, and partly in consideration of their reverend beards, which so notably distinguish them from all other creatures. The staid yet energetic horse has the suffrage for the mayoralty and other civil dignitaries. Estate owners and peasants are serpents, moles, rats and mice. The ass, on account of his braying voice, is always the leader of the church-choir. Treasurers, cashiers and inspectors are commonly wolves; their clerks, being hawks. The (roosters) cocks are appointed for watchmen, and the dogs house-porters.

The first who came on board of us, was a lean wolf or inspector, the same as a custom-house-officer in Europe, followed by four hawks, his clerks. These took

OUR HOLLOW EARTH

from our wares what pleased them best, proving to us thereby that they understood their business perfectly, and had all its appropriate tricks at their fingers' ends. The captain took me ashore with him. As soon as we had set foot on the quay, a cock came towards us, demanded whence we were, the nature of our cargo, and announced us to the inspector-general. This latter received us with much courtesy, and invited us to dine with him. The mistress of the house, whom I had heard to be one of the greatest beauties among the female wolves, was not present at the table: the reason of this was, as we afterwards learned, her husband's jealousy, who did not deem it advisable to allow such a handsome wife to be seen by strangers. There were, however, several ladies at table; among others, a certain commodore's wife, a white cow with black spots: next to her sat a black cat, wife to the master of hunt at court, newly arrived from the country. At my side was placed a speckled sow, the lady of a renovation-inspector: that species of officership being generally taken from the hog-race. It must be observed that the inhabitants of the Mezendoric empire, although they are animals in figure, have hands and fingers on the fore feet.

After dinner the speckled sow entered into conversation with our interpreter, during which she told him that she was overhead and ears in love with me. He comforted her in the best manner he could, and promised her his support and aid; then he turned himself towards me and endeavored to persuade me to be easy; but when he observed that his flattering and arguments were vain, he advised me to take to flight, as he knew that this lady would move heaven and earth to satisfy her desires. From this time I remained constantly on board; but the ship itself was not a fortification sufficiently secure from the attacks of this lady, who by messengers and love-letters strove to melt the ice that surrounded my heart. Had I not, in the shipwreck I afterwards suffered, lost my papers, I should now give some specimens of the swine's poetry. I have forgotten it all, except the following lines, in which she praises her being thus:

O thou! for whom my too fond soul most ardently doth thirst, For whom my earliest passion, in retirement I have nursed: Think not my figure homely, though it be endued in bristles,— What beauty hath the leafless tree, through which the cold wind whistles? How unadorned the noble horse, when of his beauteous mane he's shorn! O! who would love a purring cat, all in her furlessness forlorn. Ah, look around my darling pig! look on all living things, From the huge unwieldy mammoth to the smallest bird that sings;— Were these not shagged or feathered all, how loudly should we jeer;— Who would warmly strive to please e'en man, were man without a beard?

After our truck was finished and a rich freight stowed away, we sailed for home. We had scarcely got into the open sea when it suddenly became calm, but soon after the wind breezed up. Having sailed awhile with a good wind, we saw again some mermaids, who

OUR HOLLOW EARTH

—dripping wet Shot forth, and dived between the foaming waves,

and now and then emitted horrible shrieks. The sailors were much terrified at this, for they knew by experience, that these mournful sounds were presages of storm and wreck. They had scarcely taken in the sails, before the whole heavens became veiled in black clouds:

Day sinks in night: all nature shudders. Then, in an instant, loose from every point The storm, in frightful gusts and devilish uproar Breaks; the axis of the globe grates fearful,— And thunders, clap on clap, resound the concave: The waves, din-maddened, tower to mountains. Wildly, gone her helm, the half-crushed craft Tumbles ungovernable. Now despairing shrieks Mingling with ocean's roar and crash of heaven, Rise from the peopled deck: 'tis finished!

Every movable thing on deck floated off, for besides the ever-rolling billows, an immense rain fell in terrific water-spouts, accompanied by thunder and lightning. It seemed as though all the elements had conspired for our destruction. During the rolling of the ship, our masts were carried away, and then all hope of salvation was gone. Now and then a huge billow rolled over us, and carried with it one or two men far beyond the ship. The storm raged more and more; no one cared longer for the vessel: without helm, without masts, without captain and mates, who had been washed overboard, the wreck lay at the pleasure of the waves. Having floated thus for three days, a bauble for the storm, we finally descried a mountainous land in the distance.

While rejoicing in the hope of soon reaching this haven, our vessel struck so hard against a blind rock, that she was instantly dashed in pieces. In the confusion and terror of the moment I got hold of a plank, and, careless for the rest, thought only upon saving myself, so that even now I know nothing of the fate of my companions. I was quickly driven forth by the billows; and this was fortunate for me, for otherwise I should have been crushed among the timbers of the ship or torn in pieces by the jagged rocks upon which we had been cast, or escaping this should eventually have perished from hunger and fatigue.

I was wafted by the waves within a cape, where the sea was calmer, and where the roaring of the excited ocean sounded less frightfully. When I saw that I was near the shore, I began to scream vigorously, hoping to call the inhabitants to my assistance. I soon heard a sound on the seashore, and saw some of the natives come from a wood near by; they got into a yawl and sailed towards me; this boat being curiously fashioned of ozier and oak-branches twisted together, I concluded that this people must be very wild and uncultivated. I was heartily glad, when I found them to be men, for they were the first human beings I had met during the whole voyage. They are very like the inhabitants of our globe, who live in hot climates; their beards are black and their hair curled; the few among them who have long and light hair, are considered monsters.

OUR HOLLOW EARTH

The land which they inhabit is very rocky: from the curved ridges of the rocks and the connecting tops of the mountains, which cut the air in multiplied sinuosities, every sound reverberates in echo upon echo from the dales below. The people in the yawl approached the plank upon which I floated, drew me from it, carried me to the shore, and gave me to eat and drink. Although the food did not taste very good, yet as I had fasted for three days, it refreshed me very much, and in a short time I regained my former strength.

CHAPTER XII.

THE AUTHOR'S ARRIVAL IN QUAMA.

Meanwhile a large multitude of people collected around me from all parts. They requested me to speak; but as I did not understand their language I could not answer them. They repeated often the word Dank, Dank, and supposing them to be Germans, I addressed them in this language, then in Danish, and finally in Latin; but they signified to me, by shaking their heads, that these languages were unknown to them. I tried at last to declare myself in the subterranean tongues, namely, in Nazaric and Martinianic; but it was in vain.

After having addressed each other, thus incomprehensibly for a long time, I was carried to a small hut, formed of wickers intricately twisted. In this hut were neither chairs nor tables; these people seat themselves on the ground to eat; instead of beds they spread straw on the earthy floor, upon which they throw themselves indiscriminately at night. Their food is milk, cheese, barley-bread and meat, which they rudely broil on the coals; for they do not understand cooking. Thus I lived with them, like a dog, until I learned so much of their language, that I could speak with them and assist them a little in their ignorance.

The simplest rules of living that I prepared for them were considered as divine commands. My fame soon spread abroad, and all the villages around sent forth crowds to a teacher, who, they believed, had been sent to them from heaven. I heard even, that some had commenced a new chronology from the date of my arrival. All this pleased me only so much the more, as formerly in Nazar I had been abused for my imprudence and wavering judgment, and in Martinia despised and commiserated for my ignorance.

True, indeed, is the old proverb; that among the blind the one-eyed rules. I had now come to a land, where with little understanding, I could raise myself to the highest dignities. There were here the best opportunities to employ my talents, since this fruitful land produced in abundance whatever subserved for pleasure and luxury as well as usefulness and comfort. The inhabitants were not indocile nor were they wanting in conception; but since they had been blessed with no light without themselves, they groped in the thickest darkness.

OUR HOLLOW EARTH

When I told them of my birth, my native land, of the shipwreck I had suffered, and of other occurrences in my voyages, not one would credit me. They thought rather that I was an inhabitant of the sun, and had come down to enlighten them, wherefore they called me Pikil-Su, that is the sun's ambassador. For their religion, they believed in and acknowledged a God, but cared not at all to prove his existence. They thought it enough for them that their forefathers had believed the same; and this blind submission to time-honored formul was their simple and sole theology.

Of the moral law, they were ignorant of all commandments save this: Do not unto others that which you would not have others do unto you. They had no laws; the will of the emperor was their only rule. Of chronology they had but a slight conception; their years were determined by the eclipses of the sun by Nazar's intervention. Were one asked his age, he would answer: that he had attained so many eclipses. Their knowledge of natural science too, was very unsatisfactory and unreasonable; they believed the sun to be a plate of gold, and the planet Nazar, a cheese. Their property consisted in hogs, which, after marking, they drove into the woods: the wealth of each was determined by the number of his swine.

I applied myself, with all the fervor imaginable, to refine and enlighten this rude, yet promising people, so that shortly I came to be regarded among them as a saint; their trust in my wisdom was so great, that they thought nothing impossible with me. Therefore, when overtaken by misfortune, they would hasten to my hut and pray for my assistance. Once I found a peasant on his knees before my door, weeping, and bitterly complaining over the unfruitfulness of his trees, and beseeching me to use my authority, that his trees should bear fruit to him abundantly, as of old.

I had heard that this whole country was governed by a Regent, whose residence, or palace, at that time, was about eight days' travel from the town where I lived. I say at that time, because the court dwelt, not in substantial, fixed houses, but in tents; and the residence was moved at pleasure from one province to another. The ruler at that period was an old man, named Casba, which signifies, the great emperor. In consideration of its many large provinces, this country was indeed a great empire; but, from the ignorance of the inhabitants, who made little use of their many natural advantages, and also from the absence of that unanimity among the provinces, which would have dignified and strengthened their counsels, and subserved for their mutual protection, they were exposed to the attacks and mockeries of their more vigorous neighbors, and not unfrequently obliged to pay tribute to nations much inferior to themselves.

The report of my name and power was spread in a short time even to the remotest provinces. Nothing could be done without consulting me, as an oracle, and when any undertaking miscarried, its failure was ascribed to my indifference or indignation; wherefore, oblations were frequently made to assuage my anger. Finally the rumor was carried to the ears of the old emperor, that a great man had come into his dominions, in a strange dress, who gave himself out as ambassador of the sun, and had proved himself more than man, by bestowing to the Quamites (thus the inhabitants were called, after the name of the land, Quama,) wise and almost divine rules of life.

He therefore sent ambassadors, with orders to invite me to the imperial residence. These were thirty in number, all clothed in tiger-skins, this dress being considered in Quama the greatest of ornaments, since none were permitted to wear it, but those who had distinguished themselves in war against the Tanaquites, a nation of sensible tigers, and the mortal enemies of the Quamites.

I had built, in the town where I dwelt, a walled house, after the European style. At the sight of it, the imperial ambassadors were astonished, and exclaimed that it was a work beyond human powers; they entered it, as a sanctuary, with devout reverence, and there proclaimed to me the emperor's invitation in the following speech: "Since the great emperor, our most gracious lord, reckons his genealogy through manifold generations, from Spunko, the sun's son, the primary regent of Quama, nothing could surprise him more agreeably than this embassy; wherefore his majesty joyfully greets the ambassador of the sun, and humbly invites him to the capital city of the empire." I answered by expressing my most humble thanks for the emperor's condescension, and immediately repaired, with the ambassadors, to the capital. These lords had been fourteen days on their journey to me, but assisted by my genius, the return occupied only four days.

I had observed, during my residence in this country, that there were vast numbers of horses running wild in the woods, and hence rather burthensome than useful to the inhabitants. I showed to the people how beneficial these animals might be made to them, and taught them how to tame these noble creatures. At my suggestion and by my direction, a number of them were caught and broken in, and thus I was enabled to mount the ambassadors, and materially shorten the period of our journey.

No idea can be formed of the wonder and astonishment with which the Quamites witnessed our entry into the city; some were so frightened that they ran far into the country. The emperor himself dared not, in his fear, come out from his tent, nor would he stir, until one of the ambassadors, dismounting his horse, went in and explained the whole secret to him. Shortly I was, with a great retinue, led into the imperial tent. The old emperor was seated on a carpet surrounded by his courtiers. On my entrance, I acknowledged, in the most polite terms, the exceeding grace his imperial majesty had shown me; thereupon the emperor arose and asked me what the king of the sun, and father of his family proposed to do.

Conceiving it politic, and even necessary not to undeceive the Quamites in the opinion they themselves first entertained, I answered: that his majesty, the king of the sun, had sent me down to this land to refine, by good laws and salutary rules of life, the uncultivated manners of the Quamites, and teach them the arts, through which they might not only resist and repel their valiant and energetic neighbors, but even extend the boundaries of their own empire; and added, that I had been ordered to remain with them forever.

The emperor listened to this speech with much apparent pleasure, ordered a tent to be immediately raised for me near his own, gave me fifteen servants, and treated me less as a subject than as an intimate friend.

OUR HOLLOW EARTH

CHAPTER XIII.

THE BEGINNING OF THE FIFTH MONARCHY.

From this time all my exertions were directed to the accomplishment of a radical reform throughout the country. I commenced by improving their mode of warfare, in exercising the young men in riding, fencing and shooting. My constant labor was rewarded so well that, in a short time, I exhibited before the emperor six thousand horsemen.

At this period the Tanaquites were preparing for a new attack upon the Quamites, on account of the refusal of this latter people to pay a yearly tribute which had been several times demanded and as often denied. I went, at the emperor's desire, with my cavalry and some footmen to meet the invaders. To the infantry I gave javelins and arrows, that they might fight their enemies at a distance; for the Quamites had formerly used only short swords or poignards, and consequently were obliged to meet in close combat their frightful foes, the Tanaquites, who excelling them greatly in personal strength, had great advantage over them. Hearing that the enemy were approaching the boundary, as commander-in-chief, I repaired instantly towards them.

On meeting the invaders I caused the footmen to attack them with their javelins; this put them into panic and flight, and determined the fate of the day. The enemy suffered a terrible defeat and the Tanaquitic leader, with twenty other noble tigers, were taken prisoners alive and carried in triumph to Quama. It is not possible to describe the general and tumultuous joy that filled the whole country for this glorious victory; because in former wars the Quamites had generally been obliged to lay down their arms. The emperor commanded the prisoners to be immediately executed, according to old custom; but considering this a horrible custom, I persuaded him to respite them, and put them in prison for further deliberation.

I had observed that this land was very rich in saltpetre, and had collected a considerable quantity for the purpose of making powder. This intention I had kept secret, however, from all except the emperor, whose permission I needed to establish manufactories for rifles and other guns. With the aid of these I hoped in a

133

short time to subdue all the enemies of the empire. When I had finished some hundred rifles and prepared balls suitable for them, I made a trial of my project to the astonishment of all. A certain number of soldiers were selected to learn this military art, and were exercised in the management of the guns.

When this body of soldiers had become accustomed to the use of these new engines of war, and could employ them effectively, a review was held, after which the emperor proclaimed me Jakal, that is, generalissimo over the whole army. While all these matters were pending, I had entered into an intimate friendship with the brave leader of the Tanaquites, the imprisoned Tomopoloko, with whom I held frequent and interesting conversations, with the object of learning the constitution, character, and customs of his nation. I could not but observe, to my great astonishment, that they were a witty, moral and enlightened people, and that the sciences were earnestly and effectively cultivated by them. The chief told me, that towards the east were a valorous people, against whose attacks, the Tanaquites were obliged to keep themselves always prepared. The inhabitants of that country, he added, were small, and in reality much inferior in bodily strength to those of Tanaquis; but being of superior acuteness and agility, and excellent bowmen, they had in fact, often forced the Tanaquites to sue for peace.

I soon came to know, that this formidable nation consisted of cats; and that they had distinguished themselves among all the nations under the firmament, for their rational judgment and political acumen. It provoked and pained me not a little, that skilfulness, the sciences, and polite manners, should be universally among the animals of the subterranean world, while only real human beings, namely, the Quamites were sunk to the profoundest depths of uncultivated barbarism. I consoled myself, however, in the hope that, through my endeavors, this shame would soon cease, and the Quamites would recover that dominion, which belonged to them as men over all other animals.

Since their last defeat, the Tanaquites kept very quiet for a long time; but when they found out the nature and condition of our cavalry; when they discovered that those centaurs, who had frightened them so terribly at first, were nothing in reality, but tamed horses with men seated upon them, they took courage and armed new troops against the Quamites, under the command of their king. Their whole army consisted of twenty thousand tigers, all veteran soldiers, heroes of many hard fought fields, except two regiments of new recruits; these hastily collected warriors were, however, more formidable in name and numbers than in service. Already sure of victory, they fell at once upon Quama.

I immediately ordered against them twelve thousand infantry, among whom were six hundred musketeers, and four thousand horsemen. As I had not the slightest doubt of a fortunate termination to this expedition, I requested the emperor to take command of it, and thus reap the honor of the victory. By this appearance of modesty, I lost no respect, for the whole army still considered me the true leader. I first directed my cavalry against the enemy, but these were resisted with so much vigor, that the side of victory was for a long time doubtful: at the critical moment, when triumph was vacillating between the two powers, I detached my musketeers from the main body and advanced upon the foe.

The Tanaquites were much astonished at the first shots, for they could not conceive whence came the thunder and lightning; but when they saw the mournful effects of our continued volleys, they became terrified; at the first discharge fell about two hundred tigers, among which were two chaplains, who were shot down while encouraging the soldiers to bravery. When I observed the panic among the enemy, I commanded a second discharge, whose results were more fatal than the former; their king himself was shot: then the Tanaquites took to flight; our cavalry followed them, and cut down so many of the flying multitude, that those in the rear could not proceed from the huge piles of slain that covered the way. When the battle was over, we counted the killed of the enemy and found them to be thirteen thousand: our own loss was comparatively very slight.

The victorious army marched into the kingdom of Tanaqui and encamped before its capital. The general terror had meanwhile increased so much, that the magistrates submissively met the conquerors and delivered the keys of the city. The capital surrendering, the whole country soon followed its example. The disregard and contempt in which the Quamites had to this time been held, were changed to admiration and fear: the empire, with the addition of the newly conquered kingdom, was extended to twice its former size.

The glory of these actions was with one voice ascribed to my superior knowledge and untiring industry; and the esteem which had been long cherished for me, now passed over to a reverent and divine worship. This period of general peace and exultation, I thought a fitting time to advance the civilization and refinement of the Quamites, and as a practical commencement to this great work I ordered the royal Tanaquitic library to be moved to Quama.

My curiosity to become acquainted with this library had been at first excited by the imprisoned leader Tomopoloko, who told me that among its manuscripts was one, whose author had been up to our globe, in which history of his travels he had described several of its kingdoms, particularly those of Europe. The Tanaquites had seized this manuscript during one of their predatory excursions into a distant land; but as the author had concealed his name, they knew not what countryman he was, nor in what manner he had passed up through the earth.

The quaint title of this book was: "Tanian's[2] Travels Above-ground; being a description of the kingdoms and countries there, especially those of Europe." From the antiquity of this work together with its great popularity, it had become so ragged, that what I was most anxious to learn, namely, the narration of the author's

OUR HOLLOW EARTH

journey to our earth and his return, was most unfortunately lost. Here is the contents of this singular manuscript, such as I found it:

"Fragments of Tanian's Diary, kept on a Voyage above-ground, Translated by his Excellency, M. Tomopoloko, General-in-chief, in the Service of his Tanaquitic majesty."

* * * * *

"This land (Germany) was called the Roman empire; but it has been an empty title, since the Roman monarchy was demolished several centuries since. The language of this land is not easy to understand, on account of its perverted style; for, what in other languages is placed before, in this comes after, so that the meaning cannot be had before a whole page is read through. The form of government is very inconsistent; some think they have a regent and yet have none; it should be an empire, yet it is divided into several duchies, each of which has its own government, and often engages in a formal war with its neighbor.

The whole land is called 'holy,' although there is not to be found in it the least trace of piety. The regent, or more correctly the unregent, who bears the name of emperor, is denominated 'the continual augmenter of his country,' although he not seldom diminishes it; 'invincible,' notwithstanding he is often slain: sometimes by the French, sometimes by the Turks. One has no less reason to wonder at the people's rights and liberties; but although they have many rights, they are forbidden to use them. Innumerable commentaries have been written upon the German constitution, but notwithstanding this, they have made no advance because

* * * * *

"The capital of this country (France) is called Paris, and is very large, and may in a certain degree be considered the capital of all Europe; for it exercises a peculiar law-giving power over the whole continent. It has, for example, the exclusive right to prescribe the universal mode of dress and living; and no style of dress, however inconvenient or ridiculous, may be controverted after the Parisians have once established it. How or when they obtained this prescriptive right is unknown to me. I observed, however, that this dominion did not extend to other things; for the other nations often make war with the French, and not seldom force them to sue for peace on very hard terms; but subservience in dress and living nevertheless continues. In quickness of judgment, inquisitiveness after news, and fruitfulness of discovery, the French are much like the Martinians.

* * * * *

"From Bologna we went to Rome. This latter city is governed by a priest, who is held to be the mightiest of the kings and rulers of Europe, although his possessions may be travelled through in one day. Beyond all other regents, who only have supremacy over their subjects' lives and goods, he can govern souls. The Europeans generally believe that this priest has in his possession the keys of heaven. I was very curious to see these keys, but all my endeavors were in vain. His power, not only over his own subjects, but the whole human race, consists principally in that he can absolve those whom God condemns, and condemn those whom God absolves; an immense authority, which the inhabitants of our subterranean world seriously believe is not becoming to any mortal man.

But it is an easy matter to induce the Europeans to credit the most unreasonable assertions, and submit to the most high-handed assumptions, notwithstanding they consider themselves alone sensible and enlightened, and, puffed up with their foolish conceits, look contemptuously upon all other nations, whom they call barbarous.

"I will not, by any means, defend our subterranean manners and institutions: my purpose simply is, to examine those of the Europeans, and show how little claim these people have to find fault with other nations.

"It is customary, in some parts of Europe, to powder the hair and clothes with ground and sifted corn; the same which nature has produced for the nourishment of man. This flour is called hair-powder. It is combed out with great care at night, preparatory to a fresh sprinkling in the morning. There is another custom with them, which did not appear less ridiculous to me. They have certain coverings for the head, called hats, made ostensibly, to protect the head from the weather, but which, instead of being used for this very reasonable purpose, are generally worn under the arm, even in the winter. This seemed as foolish to me as would the instance of one's walking through the city with his cloak or breeches in his hand; thus exposing his body, which these should cover, to the severity of the weather.

"The doctrines of European religion are excellent and consistent with sound reason. In their books of moral law they are commanded to read the Christian precepts often; to search into their true meaning, and are advised to be indulgent with the weak and erring. Nevertheless, should any understand one or another doctrine of these books in any but the established sense, they would be imprisoned, lashed, yes, and even burned for their want of judgment. This seemed to me the same case, as if one should be punished for a blemish in sight, through which he saw that object square which others believed to be round. I was told that some thousand people had been executed by hanging or burning, for their originality of thought.

"In most cities and villages are to be found certain persons standing in high places, who animadvert severely upon the sins of others, which they themselves commit daily: this seemed to me as sensible as the preaching of temperance by a drunkard.

"In the larger towns, it is almost generally the fashion to invite one's guests, immediately after meals, to imbibe a kind of sup made from burnt beans, which they call coffee. To the places where this is drunk, they are drawn in a great box on four wheels, by two very strong animals; for the higher classes of Europeans hold it to be very indecent to move about on their feet.

"On the first day of the year, the Europeans are attacked by a certain disease, which we subterraneans know nothing of. The symptoms of this malady are a peculiar disturbance of the mind and agitation of the head; its effects are that none can remain, on that day, five minutes in one place. They run furiously from one house to another, with no appreciable reason. This disease continues with many even fourteen days; until at last, they become weary of their eternal gadding, check themselves and regain their former health.

"In France, Italy and Spain, the people lose their reason for some weeks, in the winter season. This delirium is moderated by strewing ashes on the foreheads of the sufferers. In the northern parts of Europe, to which this disease sometimes extends, and where the ashes have no power, nature is left to work the cure.

"It is the custom with most Europeans, to enter into a solemn compact with God, in the presence of witnesses, three or four times a year, which they invariably and immediately break. This compact is called 'communion,' and seems to have been established only to show that the Europeans are used to break their promises several times each year. They confess their sins and implore the mercy of God, in certain melodies, accompanied by instrumental music. As the magnitude of their sins increases, their music becomes louder: thus fluters, trumpeters and drummers are favorite helpers to devotion.

"Almost all the nations of Europe are obliged to acknowledge and believe in the doctrines, which are contained in a certain 'holy book.' At the south the reading of this book is entirely forbidden; so that the people are forced to credit what they dare not read; in these same regions, it is likewise austerely forbidden to worship God, except in a language incomprehensible to the people; so that, only those prayers are held to be lawful and pleasing to God, which are uttered from memory, without comprehension.

"The learned controversies which occupy the European academies, consist in the discussion of matters, the development of which is productive of no benefit, and in the examination of phenomena, the nature of which is beyond the reach of the human mind. The most serious study of a European scholar, is the consideration of a pair of old boots, the slippers, necklaces and gowns of a race long extinct. Of the sciences, both worldly and divine, none judge for themselves, but subscribe blindly to the opinions of a few. The decisions of these, when once established, they cling to, like oysters to the rocks. They select a few from their number whom they call, 'wise,' and credit them implicitly. Now, there would be nothing to object against this, could raw and ignorant people decide in this case; but to decide concerning wisdom requires, methinks, a certain degree of sapience in the judge.

OUR HOLLOW EARTH

"In the southern countries, certain cakes are carried about, which the priests set up for Gods; the most curious part of this matter is, the bakers themselves, while the dough yet cleaves to their fingers, will swear that these cakes have created heaven and earth.

"The English prefer their liberty to all else, and are not slaves, except to their wives. Today they reject that religion, which yesterday they professed. I ascribe this fickleness to the situation of their country; they are islanders and seamen, and probably become affected by the variable element that surrounds them. They inquire very often after each other's health, so that one would suppose them to be all doctors; but the question: how do you do? is merely a form of speech; a sound without the slightest signification.

"Towards the north, is a republic, consisting of seven provinces. These are called 'united,' notwithstanding there is not to be found the least trace of union among them. The mob boast of their power, and insist upon their right to dispose of state affairs; but no where is the commonalty more excluded from such matters; the whole government being in the hands of some few families.

"The inhabitants of this republic heap up great riches with anxious and unwearied vigilance, which, however, they do not enjoy: their purses are always full, their stomachs always empty. One would almost believe they lived on smoke, which they continually suck through tubes or pipes, made of clay. It must, nevertheless, be confessed, that these people surpass all others in cleanliness; for they wash everything but their hands.

"Every land has its own laws and customs, which are usually opposed to each other. For example; by law, the wife is subject to the husband; by custom, the husband is ruled by the wife.

"In Europe, the superfluous members of society only are respected; these devour not only the fruits of the land but the land itself. The cultivators of the soil, who feed these gorges are degraded for their industry and despised for their usefulness.

"The prevalence of vice and crime in Europe may perhaps be fairly inferred from the great number of gallows and scaffolds to be seen everywhere. Each town has its own executioner. I must, for justice sake, clear England from this stigma; I believe there are no public murderers in that country: the inhabitants hang themselves.

"I have a kind of suspicion that the Europeans are cannibals; for they shut large flocks of healthful and strong persons in certain inclosures, called cloisters, for the purpose of making them fat and smooth. This object seldom fails, as these prisoners, free from all labor and care, have nothing to do but to enjoy themselves in these gardens of pleasure.

"Europeans commonly drink water in the morning to cool their stomachs; this

139

object accomplished, they drink brandy to heat them again.

"In Europe are two principal sects in religion; the Roman catholic and the protestant. The protestants worship but one God; the catholics, several. Each city and village, with these, has its appropriate God or Goddess. All these deities are created by the pope, or superior priest at Rome, who, on his part, is chosen by certain other priests, called cardinals. The mighty power of these creators of the creator of the gods, does not, as it would seem to an indifferent spectator, apparently alarm the people.

"The ancient inhabitants of Italy subdued the whole world, and obeyed their wives; the present, on the contrary, abuse their wives and submit to the whole world.

"The Europeans generally feed upon the same victuals with the subterraneans. The Spaniards alone live on the air.

"Commerce flourishes here and there; many things are offered for sale in Europe, which with us are never objects of trade. Thus in Rome, people sell heaven; in Switzerland, themselves; and in * * * * * * *, the crown, sceptre and throne are offered at public auction.

"In Spain, idleness is the true mark of a well-bred man; and the distinguishing proof of pure nobility is an aptitude to sleep.

"Among European writers, those are in the highest repute, who change the natural order of words, making that which is in itself simple and distinct, intricate and incomprehensible. The class most noted for this abominable perversion of style is that of the 'poets:' this singular removal of words is called 'poetry.' The capability to puzzle is by no means the only requisite to become a true poet; one must be able to lie most terribly. A certain old poet named Homerus, who possessed both these qualities in an eminent degree, is styled the 'master,' and is idolized with a kind of divine worship. He has had many imitators of his distortion of sentences and falsification of truth; but, it is said, none have yet reached his excellence.

"The cultivators of science purchase books in great quantities, not so much, I am told, for the sake of the contents, as for their antiqueness of style or elegance of binding.

"The learned and unlearned are distinguished from each other by different dresses and manners; but especially by different religions: the latter believe mostly in one God; the former worship many divinities, both male and female. Among the principal of these are, Apollo, Minerva, and nine muses; besides many lesser whole and half Gods. The poets particularly implore their aid and 'hail' them when they take a notion to rage.

"The learned are divided, according to their different studies into the classes of philosophers, poets, grammarians, natural philosophers, metaphysicians, &c.

OUR HOLLOW EARTH

"A philosopher is a scientific tradesman, who, for a certain price, sells prescriptions of self-denial, temperance and poverty; he generally preaches the pains of wealth, till he becomes rich himself, when he abandons the world for a comfortable and dignified retreat. The father of the philosophers, Seneca, is said to have collected royal wealth.

"A poet is one who makes a great stir with printed prattle, falsehood and fury. Madness is the characteristic of the true poet. All those who express themselves, with clearness, precision and simplicity are deemed unworthy of the laurel wreath.

"The grammarians are a sort of military body, who disturb the public peace. They are distinguished from all other warriors, by dress and weapons. They wear black instead of colored uniforms, and wield pens rather than swords. They fight with as much obstinacy for letters and words as do the others for liberty and fa-ther-land.

"A natural philosopher is one who searches into the bowels of the earth, studies the nature of animals, worms and insects, and, in a word, is familiar with every thing, but himself.

"A metaphysician is a sort of philosopher, partly visionary and partly sceptical, who sees what is concealed from all others. He describes the being and unfolds the nature of souls and spirits, and knows both what is, and what is not. From the acuteness of his sight, the metaphysician cannot discern what lies directly before his feet.

"I have thus briefly considered the condition of the learned republic in Europe. I could relate many other things, but I think I have given the reader a sufficient test, by which he may judge how far the Europeans have a right to hold themselves preminent for wisdom.

"The people above-ground are exceedingly pious, and extraordinarily zealous in praying. Their prayers, however, do not arise from the impulses and emotions of their hearts; but are subdued to mere matters of form, directed by bells, clocks or sun-dials. Their devotion is entirely mechanical, founded on external signs and old customs rather than in sincere feeling.

"When I came to Italy, I fancied myself master over the whole country; for every one called himself my slave. I took a notion to test the extent of this humble obedience, and commanded my landlord to lend me his wife for a night; he became very angry, however, at this, and ordered me out of his house.

"In the north, there are many people who seek with great pains to obtain titles of offices which they do not hold; and many lose their reason in their eagerness to be on the right side. Furthermore,"

*　*　*　*　*

Here I lost my patience. Inflamed to the utmost fury, I threw the book on the ground, and assured Tomopoloko, who was by me, that it was the fiction of an unjust and choleric writer. When my first passion was cooled, I reviewed my sentence, and finally concluded that the author of these travels, although unfair and untrue in many particulars, had nevertheless made some good points and happy reflections.

I will now return to civil affairs. All our neighbors had kept very quiet for a long period, and during this peace I made every effort to constitute the government according to my own notions, and strengthen the army in numbers and efficiency.

Suddenly, we received information that three warlike and formidable nations, namely, the Arctonians, Kispusiananians and Alectorians, had united against the Quamites. The first named were bears gifted with reason and speech. The Kispusiananians were a nation of large cats celebrated for their cunning and ferocity. The Alectorians were cocks, armed with bows and arrows. These arrows with poisoned tips, were cast with wonderful precision, and their least touch was fatal.

These three nations had been irritated by the uncommon progress of the Quamites as well as by the fall of the Tanaquites. The allied powers sent ambassadors to Quama, to demand the liberty of the imprisoned Tanaquitians and the cession of their land, with power to declare war should the same be denied. By my advice, they were immediately dismissed with the following answer: "Since the Tanaquitians, violators of peace and alliance, have deserved the misery which they have brought upon themselves by their own folly and pride, his majesty, the emperor, is determined to defend, to the utmost, the possessions of a land, conquered in a lawful war, in spite of the threats and fearless of the strength of your unnatural alliance."

In a short time I had an army of forty thousand men ready for the coming war: among these were eight thousand horsemen and two thousand riflemen. The emperor, old as he was, determined to follow this campaign; his eagerness and ambition were so great, that neither his wife's representations nor mine were effective enough to induce him to abandon this intention.

In this state of affairs, I was made somewhat uneasy from mistrust of the Tanaquitians. I feared that, impatient of their unaccustomed slavery, they would take the first opportunity to throw off their yoke, and go over to the enemy. I did not deceive myself; for immediately after the declaration of war, we heard that full twelve thousand Tanaquitians in complete armor, had marched for the enemy's encampment. Thus were we occupied at once with four mighty foes.

In the beginning of the month Kilian, we commenced our march. From a spy, we learnt that the united troops had already besieged the fort Sibol in Tanaqui, on the borders of Kispusianania. On our arrival before the place, they abandoned the siege and prepared to meet us. The battle took place in a dale near the fort, and is to this day called the "Sibolic battle."

The Arctonians, who formed their left wing, made great havoc among our cavalry; and, supported by the rebellious Tanaquites, fell furiously on our right; a moment longer and the fate of the conflict would have been determined. I detached a body of riflemen to engage the attention of the enemy, and allow the cavalry to recover; this movement was very effective; the men handled their guns well, and the enemy hastily abandoned their ground, under a terrific shower of balls. Meanwhile, the Kispusiananians on the other side pressed our infantry very hard; six hundred Quamites were down: some killed, others mortally wounded. The recovered cavalry now rushed upon them impetuously, broke their ranks, and, unresisted, slaughtered them by thousands.

The Alectorians, who formed the reserve, gave us the greatest trouble, for when our soldiers would attack them, they flew into the air, whence they shot on our heads their poisoned arrows. One of these entered the neck of the old emperor, while fighting vigorously in the midst of the field. He fell directly from his horse, was carried to his tent, and shortly after expired. The soldiers having been kept in ignorance of their sovereign's death, the battle was continued until midnight. I soon found that our balls had but little effect upon our flying enemies; their motions being so rapid that our gunners could take no aim. Some new method must be devised to check them; a lucky expedient occurred to me; I ordered the guns to be loaded with small shot: these scattering, brought them down in great flocks, and soon half of them were destroyed; the rest laid down their weapons and surrendered. The Arctonians and Kispusiananians quickly followed their example, and their fortifications were surrendered to our hands.

When all these things were fortunately brought to an end, Behold then I called together the first among the people, the eldest, The heads of all the troops, to Council, in full assembly; Like the bubbling ocean's high-roaring billows They all did stream to me; and silently heard my speech:

"Noble, brave and celebrated warriors. I doubt not, that it is well known to the most of you, that I ofttimes advised his majesty not to hazard his precious life in this desperate strife. But his natural courage and fearless heroism would not suffer him to remain at home, while his brave people exposed themselves abroad. O, that he could have witnessed our glorious victory! Then our entrance into the imperial residence would have been a true triumph, and our joy over so many noble deeds would have been perfect; not as now, mingled with tormenting sorrow! I can no longer conceal from you the mournful event, which has given each one of us, a greater wound than could all the arrows of the enemy. Know then, that our emperor, in the thickest of the battle, was struck by an unfortunate arrow, and soon after expired. Horrible event!

What sorrow, what general mourning will the loss of this great king cause over the whole country! Yet, do not lose courage! The great hero has ceased to live in himself; but he is not dead to you! Your emperor lives again in two princes, true images of their great father, and heirs no less to his virtues than to his dignities. You have not changed your emperor, but only your emperor's name. Since the prince Timuso, as the first born, receives the crown, I am, from this moment, under his sceptre, the leader of the army.

"Hail, Timuso! To him let us swear allegiance! To him, let us swear eternal loyalty! Him, let us all hereafter obey!"

OUR HOLLOW EARTH

CHAPTER XIV.
THE AUTHOR BECOMES A MONARCH UNDER THE GROUND.

When my speech was ended, they all cried out with loud voices: "We will have Pikil-Su, for emperor." When I heard this, I became terrified, and begged them, with tears in my eyes, not to forget the fidelity and duty they owed to the imperial family. But my words were of no use. They all approached me, and placed the crown upon my head, repeating the above-mentioned exclamation. I was then carried from the tent and proclaimed before the whole army, emperor of Quama, king of Tanaqui, Arctonia and Alectoria, and duke of Kispusianania. Afterwards we made a triumphal entry into the capital, where prince Timuso, himself acknowledged me for emperor. Thus, from a miserable, shipwrecked wretch, I became a great and powerful monarch. I soon married the daughter of the deceased emperor, for the people still loved and honored the old royal family. This princess was named Ralac, and

Bloomed, like the new-blown rose In mellowed, purple-smile.

when I had reduced to order the affairs of the empire, and firmly established myself on the throne, I thought of new means, by which I might extend my dominions, and render my power fearful to the whole subterranean world. I turned my attention to a navy, and soon had a fleet of twenty ships on the sea.

I soon came to regard myself an under-ground Alexander; and determined to make myself as famous as he had on our globe. I concluded to sail first for Mezendore and thence to Martinia. We set sail at that period of the year, when the planet Nazar is of the middle size, and in a few days came in sight of the Mezendoric coast.

I immediately sent ambassadors to the imperial residence, of whom was demanded in the name of the emperor,

"What their purpose; whence they came Over the foaming billows of the swelling main."

The ambassadors answered:

"Neither misleading stars, deluding winds nor storm Here brought us; with voluntary will we steered."

and thereupon delivered to the emperor a letter of the following contents:

"We, Niels Klim, ambassador of the sun, emperor in Quama, king of Tanaqui, Arctonia, and Alectoria, and duke of Kispusianania, salute the emperor of Mezendore, Miklopolata. We humbly make known, that it is concluded in the unchangeable councils of heaven, that all the empires and kingdoms of the world must surrender themselves to the power of Quama; and as the will of providence is irrevocable, your kingdom must necessarily submit to fate.

We therefore advise you to surrender voluntarily yourself and your dominions, rather than foolishly resist our invincible phalanx, and thereby experience all the bloody horrors of war.

"Given from our fleet, the third day in the month Rimat."

In a few days our ambassadors returned with a bold and haughty answer. I made a descent upon the coast, placed my army in battle array, and sent spies to examine the condition of the enemy. The spies came back in great haste, and related that an immense army, of sixty thousand in number, consisting of lions, tigers, elephants, bears and birds of prey, was drawing towards us. We were soon apprised of their near approach, by roars, shrieks and terrific cries, commingling a devilish tumult. The combat soon commenced, and truly, 'twas one of the hottest and most contumaceous, in which I ever engaged: at last we put them to flight.

In this engagement fell thirty-three thousand Mezendarians, and about four thousand were made prisoners. We followed our victory, and drew before the capital city; this we besieged both by land and sea. So energetic was our blockade, that the enemy quickly proposed a parley, and sent ambassadors to ask for peace on reasonable conditions. The emperor offered to me his daughter, the handsomest of the lionesses, in marriage, and the half of his empire as a dowry. These conditions, although very honorable, were very displeasing to me, for I considered it both unsafe and illicit to forsake my wife, whom I left behind in pregnancy, and marry a lioness. I therefore sent back the ambassadors without answer.

I now ordered my cannon to be directed against the wall, which, although built of stone, was soon rent. The emperor lost all hope and surrendered himself together with all his lands. After putting a garrison in the capital, I took the emperor on board my own ship, and laid my course for Martinia, the coast of which we reached after a long but fortunate voyage.

We obtained here the same success as elsewhere. When the Martinians submitted, I determined to include their neighbors under the same yoke. As I was preparing to effect this, ambassadors from four adjacent countries arrived, and voluntarily acknowledged allegiance to me. I now possessed so many kingdoms, that I did not deem it worth my trouble to ascertain the names of these; but included them all under the title of the Martinianic "dominion."

OUR HOLLOW EARTH

CHAPTER XV.

A SUDDEN CHANGE IN THE FORTUNES OF THE AUTHOR.

Having made so many and extraordinary warlike excursions, and added to our fleet a number of Martinianic ships, we set sail for our own land, into which we entered with a splendor exceeding the old Roman triumphs. And really my deeds deserved all possible honors; for what heroic action could be greater and more glorious than to change a despised nation, a nation exposed to the insults of its weaker neighbors, to the acknowledged and respected ruler of the whole subterranean world? What could be more honorable to a man, than to reinstate the human race in that dominion, which nature has given to it, over all other animals?

From this time a new period may be reckoned in history; a fifth monarchy can be added to the glorious roll of splendid empires. To the Assyrian, Persian, Greek and Roman empires, the Subterranean-Quamatic monarchy, which unquestionably exceeds them all in magnificence and power, may not be considered unworthy to be joined. I could not decline, for obvious reasons, the title of Koble, or great, with which the conquered nations saluted me.

I was hailed thereafter, by the following titles: "Niels the Great, Ambassador of the Sun, Emperor in Quama and Mezendore, King of Tanaqui, Alectoria, Arctonia, the Mezendoric and Martinianic dominions, Grand Duke of Kispusianania, Ruler of Martinia, etc. etc."

——firmly founded, stood The mighty empire; the favorite of fortune, I seemed as firmly fixed; not one, alas! May be deemed happy 'till his latest hour.

When I had reached this splendid and powerful height, greater than any man should desire, I became, what men usually become, who are raised from a simple state to great honor in the world. I forgot my former condition, and inclined to vanity. Instead of exerting myself to retain the favor of the people, I proved myself cruel and rigorous to all classes. My subjects, whom I had formerly endeared by friendly and polite conduct, I now regarded and treated as slaves. For this course, I came soon to be despised; the love and reverence of my people were changed to indifference and fear. Their sentiments towards me I soon had reason to understand, when I issued a proclamation to the inhabitants.

OUR HOLLOW EARTH

The occasion was this: the empress, whom I left in pregnancy during my last expedition, had in my absence been delivered of a son. This prince I wished to have nominated as my successor. I therefore summoned a Diet, and commanded the Quamitian nobles and the great men among the conquered nations, to meet in the capital, at the crowning of the child. None dared to disobey this proclamation, and the coronation passed off with great magnificence; but I observed by the countenances of my subjects, that their joy was dissembled. I became more confirmed in my mistrust, when I learnt that a multitude of libels had been spread about. These libels, by unknown authors, criticised me very severely, and asserted that prince Timuso was insulted in the choice of my son.

This enraged me so much that I could not rest until that noble and excellent prince should be removed from my path. I therefore suborned some persons to accuse him of treason; and since rulers seldom want assistants, when they would commit crimes, I was quickly enabled to prove that Timuso had attempted my life. I had him sentenced to death by bribed judges, and then threw him into prison, where he was privately murdered; for I feared to excite a rebellion by a public execution. I had determined to murder the younger prince likewise; but postponed it. His youth procured for him the safety, which neither my justice nor humanity would have granted him. Having once imbued my hands in innocent blood, my cruelty and moroseness knew no bounds. I doomed to death several whole families, whose loyalty I merely suspected. Not a day passed without bloodshed. I defiled my soul with the blood of innocence, virtue and nobleness. All these things hastened a rebellion, excited by the nobles, who had been long disgusted with me.

I will here acknowledge, that I deserved all the misfortunes that afterwards met me. It had certainly been more fit for a Christian king to have taught his ignorant and heathen subjects to know the true God, and to have given them an example in my own person of the sweet charities of the true religion, than to have excelled, even themselves in barbarity, sin and moral turpitude. It would have been an easy matter for me to have reformed the whole subterranean world, for whatever I commanded was fulfilled; whatever I determined was received in perfect good faith; whenever I spoke, my words were as those of a God. But I forgot God and myself; I thought of nothing but empty and vain splendor, and the augmentation of my power; wherefore I perpetrated many cruelties, until the people, unable to bear more, (and they were a patient people,) broke out against me.

While matters stood thus, I determined to lay hands on prince Hidoba. This intention I revealed to my high-chancellor, Kalak, in whom I had great confidence. He promised to be of service to me in all things, and departed to fulfil my order: but at heart, he detested my cowardly fears, and left me only to discover my plot to the prince. Together they repaired to the fort, collected the garrison, and represented, in a touching manner, their danger and my fears. The tears of the unfortunate prince gave weight to his words; all seized their arms, and promised that they would hazard their lives for him. The cunning chancellor took the opportunity to persuade them to swear loyalty to the prince, and sent messages to others, who, he knew, were displeased with me, to take arms against the tyrant.

All armed themselves, whose hearts, through fear and horror, Did burn towards their country's tyrant; they met

and united with the garrison, while I awaited the return of the chancellor.

*   *   *   *   *

By the advice of Pomopoloko, I fled seasonably to Tanaqui, leaving my own capital before the inhabitants generally were apprised of the immediate cause of the sudden out-break. Arrived in Tanaqui, I quickly collected an army of forty thousand men, and boldly retraced the steps which a few days before I had pursued in fear and trembling. I had little doubt that my powers would be augmented by Quamites, who had been either too remote to suffer from my cruelty, or too indifferent to my infamy, to hesitate in joining a force so overpowering, and a leader whose prospects were so brilliant as mine. But I was deceived in my hopes: instead of auxiliaries a herald from the prince met me. The object of his mission was to declare a formal war, and, for a commencement of hostilities, that my wife and son had been imprisoned. On the footsteps of the herald came the Quamitic forces. A bloody engagement took place, in which our part proved to be inferior. I, left to my fate, fled to a neighboring mountain, crossed its side and descended to a dale behind it.

There I remained in concealment for some time, bemoaning, the while, my misery, as I then believed, but which I afterwards more justly named, my folly. I was so agitated, had so thoroughly lost that presence of mind for which I had in former days been distinguished, that I did not remove from my head the crown, which, being ornamented with sunbeams, would have easily betrayed me. While panting like a bayed lion, I heard a nestling on the other side of the mountain, which I supposed was made by men beating the bushes to discover any hiders. I now looked around for a more secure retreat, for I doubted not that my flight had been noticed, and that these pursuers would search on my side of the mountain. Behind me was

——A thick and matted forest, sunk between hills All desolate and bare, whose dark and awful silence Beckoned me.

I hurried thither, fiercely flinging aside the thorny bushes that clung as fiercely to me, and came at last to the mouth of a cave. Creeping in, I observed that the cave was deep, and as far as the light penetrated, level. I determined to explore its recesses, though I think I should not have been so hardy in my days of fortune.

After treading cautiously a hundred paces, I suddenly lost my footing, and plunged with the quickness of lightning, into a hole that must have had perpendicular sides.

Having shot through this passage, the abode of palpable darkness and night, I suddenly perceived a faint light.

As when through clouds the moon doth gleam With pallid smile.

As this light increased, my speed decreased, so that without pain or trouble, I was soon brought to a stand between two high mountains. My sensations, during this remarkable passage, were similar to those experienced while tossing among the billows of the ocean. On recovering, I found myself, to my great astonishment, in the same spot from which, years before, I had plunged into the subterranean regions. A moment's reflection gave me the means to account for the decrease of speed in the latter part of my course. The weight of the atmosphere is much greater on the surface of the globe, than below; consequently I was buoyed up by the increasing resistance of the air towards the surface. Had this not been the case, I should, unquestionably, at least in my own mind, have shot off to the moon.

Still, being obnoxious to cavil, I will defer this hypothesis to the astronomer's closer examination.

OUR HOLLOW EARTH

CHAPTER XVI.

THE AUTHOR'S RETURN TO HIS FATHER-LAND, AND THE END OF THE FIFTH MONARCHY.

Although perfectly sensible, my limbs were entirely benumbed; and I lay helpless for a long time. Meanwhile I ruminated on my singular course. The events of the past years rose one after another with clearness in my mind; particularly those of my exaltation and fame. Here was I, the late founder of the splendid fifth monarchy, metamorphosed to a poor and hungry bachelor-of-arts; a change so terrible and unprecedented, that it might well have disturbed the strongest brain. I seriously examined my present circumstances—were they real? or did I dream? Alas? the tremors of terror and uncertainty only gave place to the pangs of sorrow and regret.

"Almighty Father!" I exclaimed, and towards heaven Stretched my trembling hands, "what sin provoked thy vengeance, That all thy thunders crash upon my head? Where am I? whence came I? how shall I escape Thy anger."

Truly! should one look over the journals of all times, he will neither in ancient nor modern history find a parallel to so great a fall; with the single exception of that of Nebuchadnezzar, who from the greatest of kings was changed to a dumb beast.

I began to descend the mountain by the path which leads to Sandvig. When about half way down, I observed some boys, whom I beckoned towards me, repeating the words: Jeru pikal salim, which in the Quamitic language signify: show me the way. The lads, however, were apparently frightened at seeing a man in a strange dress, and with a hat on his head glittering with golden rays; for they rushed down the mountain in great haste, arriving at Sandvig an hour before me. The rumor of the strange appearance on the mountain was spread about and caused terror throughout the town; the notion was, that the shoemaker of Jerusalem wandered among the mountains. This impression arose thus: the boys on being questioned by the townsmen, replied that I had told them who I was. I afterwards learnt that my words, Jeru pikal salim, had been interpreted by sound, and that this clew, acted upon by fear and superstition, had been developed into the strang-

OUR HOLLOW EARTH

est of fables. This story was unquestioned by this simple people, inasmuch as the adventures of the travelling shoemaker were then newly reported, and it had been asserted that he had been seen a short time before in Hamburg.

When, towards evening, I entered Sandvig, I observed that the inhabitants were collected in large flocks, to gaze at me. As I approached them and spoke, they all took to flight, except one old man: him I addressed, and begged of him to give me lodging at his house. He asked me, "where I was born, whence I came, &c." I answered him, with a sigh: "When I come to your house, I will relate events that will seem incredible to you, and whose equals you will not find in any history." The old man then took me by the hand and led me to his house. When there I demanded drink; he gave me a glass of beer. When I recovered my breath, after this draught, I addressed the old man thus: "You see before you a human being, who has been a bolt for the changing winds of fortune; one, who has been pursued by a fatality more controlling and more unhappy than was ever experienced by mortal."

"Moral and physical revolutions may be effected in a moment, without surprising men; but what has befallen me is beyond the reach of human imagination!"

"It is the traveller's fate;" my landlord answered; "many strange events and changes might happen on a voyage of sixteen hundred years."

I did not understand this, and requested him to tell me what he meant by sixteen hundred years. He replied: "If one may believe history, it is now sixteen hundred years since Jerusalem was destroyed, and I doubt not, venerable man, that you were already of age at its destruction. If what is said of you is true, you must have been born in the reign of Tiberius. I know that this matter is rather supposed than proved. The inhabitants of this place, however, believe you to be the shoemaker of Jerusalem, celebrated in history, who, since the time of Christ, has travelled about the world. Nevertheless, the more I look at you, the greater resemblance I find to an old friend of mine, who twelve years since perished on the top of a neighboring mountain."

At these words, I looked carefully at my host. In a moment the fog was cleared from before my eyes. I saw before me my dear friend Abelin, in whose house, at Bergen, I had spent many happy days. I ran to his embrace with outstretched arms. "Then 'tis you, my dear Abelin! I can scarcely believe my eyes. Here you see Klim again, who has just returned from the subterranean world. I am the same, who twelve years since plunged into the mountain cave."

He fell upon my neck and with tearful eyes, demanded where I had been and what had happened to me. I told him all that had occurred. At first he would not credit me; but afterwards he acknowledged that all must have been so, for I could never have invented such strange adventures.

OUR HOLLOW EARTH

Abelin advised me not to repeat these things to others, and to keep myself secluded in his house. He told the people, who rushed to his house to see the "shoemaker of Jerusalem," that I had vanished; for he justly concluded this to be the best and most satisfactory answer he could make to an ignorant and superstitious peasantry. I remained in concealment until clothes, more suitable to the surface of the earth, than those I brought from below, were made, when Abelin reported me to be a relative of his, lately a student in Trondhjim, on a visit.

He recommended me to the bishop of Bergen, who promised to me the first rectorship that should become vacant. This office was much to my taste, for it seemed to have a likeness to my former state, a school-master being a miniature of royalty. The rod may be likened to the sceptre; the desk to the throne. After waiting for a vacancy in vain, I determined, from necessity, to accept the first office I could get. At this time the sacristan of the church died; his place was offered to me by the bishop and accepted. An amusing promotion to one who had lately reigned over many great kingdoms. Nevertheless, since nothing is so ridiculous as poverty, and since it is foolish to throw away dirty water, before clean is at hand, I think it would have been still more laughable to have refused it. Fulfilling the duties of this office, I now live in philosophic ease.

Shortly after my induction, a marriage with a merchant's daughter was proposed to me. I could have liked the girl, but as it was probable that the empress of Quama was yet alive, I did not care to make myself obnoxious to the ban of polygamy. M. Abelin, however, into whose bosom I was used to pour my doubts, and all the pressures of my heart, abridged this fear, and advised me to marry; which I did. With this wife I have lived six years in peaceful and affectionate union. During this period she has borne me three fine sons, wholly worthy of their half brother, the prince of Quama.

To my wife, I never told my subterranean adventures; but I can never forget, for a moment, the splendor that once surrounded me. To this day, I often express myself in signs and words, which, however consistent in the mighty ruler and magnificent tyrant, are little adapted to the humble sacristan of Bergen.

THE SUPPLEMENT OF ABELIN.

Niels Klim lived to the year 1695. His irreprehensible life and amiable disposition endeared him to all. Yet were the priests now and then angry with him for his great sedateness and reservedness, which they called pride and haughtiness. I, who knew the man, wondered much at the modesty, humility and patience with which he, who had been monarch over many nations, executed his mean and vulgar duties. So long as his strength permitted, he would, at a certain time in the year, ascend the mountain and gaze into the cave, out of which he came to the surface. His friends observed that he always returned weeping, and immediately shut himself in his chamber, where he remained alone the rest of the day.

His wife informed me, that she frequently heard him murmur in his dreams, of armies and navies. His library consisted mostly of political works; for this selection he was blamed by several, who thought this description of books unfit for a sacristan.

Of the "subterranean travels," there is but a single copy, written by his own hand, which is in my possession.

I have often had it in mind to publish them, but several important reasons have hindered me from doing so.

END of Underland

Independent Publisher Of Alternative Titles Since 1965

Timothy Green Beckley's **ISSUE #50**   US $3.00

Conspiracy Journal
bizarre bazaar

Incorporating Inner Light / UFO Review

Promoting Free Speech and Individuality
Opposing The System, Censorship, Death & Taxes

IN THIS ISSUE: ▸ Strange, Amazing, Rare and Exotic Items From Worldwide Sources

A LONG AND WINDING ROAD—JOIN US ON OUR EXPLORATION OF THE UNKNOWN REALMS

"Nothing to see here. Move along please."

That's what you are usually told at the scene of an accident. But it's no accident you're receiving this publication in the mail, and there is every reason to sit back, relax and take a sip of something cold while the summer months roll along.

No one can accuse us of being a "one trick pony." We can almost guarantee that there is something within these pages for everyone. Some of you like your aliens (but do they like you?), while others are hiding in the brush waiting for Bigfoot or some other cryptid to wander by (be sure to have your camera ready). And let's not forgot those occultists, New Agers and spell crafters who love our more spiritually orientated material. Oh and hey, there are probably even a few items tucked away for those who are into more conventional Bible studies. We had a good size hit on our hands recently with Rev. Barry Downing's **"Biblical UFO Revelations,"** and Sean Casteel's **"Search For The Pale Prophet."** (They are, of course, still available — see pg 16 of our last issue, far right, second row of books for a two book special).

But hey let's jump to the present now, as we have some wonderful new titles to toot Gabriel's Horn about (don't you just cherish the way I phrase things?).

We all love our pets. They are sometimes much closer to us than our so-called friends and family. Maria D' Andrea tells us in her latest volume **"Witchcraft, The Occult And How To Select A Familiar,"** the best way to discover the importance familiars can play in our occult and witchcraft studies to bring about a world of

GEF
THE
TALKING MONGOOSE

positive benefits to the spells we cast and the rituals we perform.

Familiars can help with healing, making relationships go well, and in obtaining prosperity. They can also help the shaman do magic and dispense advice.

Witches have used them as spies thanks to their shape shifting abilities.

Now here's a pet I know you don't own. **"Gef The Talking Mongoose"** was the 8th Wonder of the World.

He lived on the Isle of Man, near the rugged coastline, could speak the Queen's English (with a few nasty words tossed in), had the abil-

Continued >

HENCHMEN
Tim Beckley, Publisher/Editor
Associates: Tim Swartz; Sean Casteel; Carol Ann Rodrigues
Layout, Graphics & Typesetting: William Kern (Adman)
CONSPIRACY JOURNAL GLOBAL COMMUNICATIONS
Payment For All Merchandise To Timothy Beckley
Box 753, New Brunswick, NJ 08903
MRUFO8@hotmail.com · PayPal Orders Preferred
All Other Methods Accepted—753-602-3407
FREE VIDEOS on our YouTube Channel
"Mr. UFOs Secret Files"
Tim Beckley

**NEW!
HELP INVESTIGATE
ONE OF THE
WORLD'S GREAT-
EST HISTORICAL
MYSTERIES**

**"TO BE OR NOT TO
BE," THAT IS THE
QUESTION.
● IS THERE
A SHAKESPEAREAN
CODE?
● WHAT IS THE
SECRET IDENTITY
OF THE BARD?**

Most of us grew up being taught that "Shakespeare" was the sole author of the greatest body of literature to have ever been created by a single person. Were we collective dupes to perhaps the most skillful fraud ever to be perpetrated on a non-suspecting populace?

Is everything we were taught about Shakespeare a cleverly orchestrated lie? The actor and grain merchant William "Shakespeare" perhaps served as a willing front for the playwright and poet whose achievements even today cannot be easily measured. Who was the real author behind the scenes, and why did he choose to conceal himself?

Order **SHAKESPEARE'S CONFIDENTIAL DOSSIER,** including Sean Casteel's "To Be Or Not To Be" plus two audio CDs narrated by Oxford scholar Stuart Robb (frequent guest on Long John Nebel Party Line and editor of "Exploring The Unknown" magazine published in the 1970s.).

☐ **All items send $20 + $5 S/H
Timothy G Beckley, Box 753, New Brunswick, NJ 08903**

**FROM CONSPIRACY JOURNAL'S "LOST VAULT"
"MY FRIEND FROM BEYOND EARTH"
— WHO WAS THE MYSTERIOUS VISITOR
WITH AMAZING POWERS?**

Minister, judge and private investigator, Rev. Frank Stranges says he met a "spaceman" inside the pentagon. Rare pamphlet describes other-worlldly experience. Plus DVD "confidential" talk and photo of "alien" suitable for framing.
**All this $20.00 + $5 S/H
Timothy Green Beckley**
Post Box 753 · New Brunswick, NJ 08903
Order direct or call 646-331-6777 and leave credit card info. Speak clearly, please.
PAYPAL to mrufo8@hotmail.com.

ity to make himself invisible and to teleport objects. He befriended an entire family and became the local gadfly. Just ask Tim Swartz who has just produced a 280 page book on this bizarre Fortean topic – one of my personal favorites!

If you are a rock 'n' roller, like many of us, you'll want to follow the exploits of the White Witch of New York. Walli Elmlark befriended the likes of David Bowie, Marc Bolan of T-Rex, Freddie Prinze Sr, and a host of other counterculture celebrities during the Seventies. And I just happened to go along for the ride. It was a wild one full of back stage parties, lots of booze, drugs and the emergence of the occult into society. Order our full color edition of **"David Bowie, UFOs, Witchcraft, Cocaine and Paranoia"** for a front row seat. Lots of color photos of your favorite rock stars by Helen Hovey to take this book over the top.

In **"Alien Strongholds on Earth,"** you will discover that "secret UFO bases exist all around us." Some are in the mountains, the deserts, under the oceans, but others could be in secluded places within driving distance of where you live. Some of the occupants lurk in the shadow world, others offer friendship and advice.

If you're looking for something a bit "stronger," we've got a new title that will scare the pants off of you — hey I promise to look the other way. **"Knife-Wielding Demons and Murderous Ghosts — Uncovering the Truth About Terrifying Homicidal Poltergeists"** is not for the weak of heart. This large format volume goes where no other book on demonology and occultism dares to tread. It seems lots of spirits are not satisfied with just going Boo.

We even have a book **"To Be Or**

Continued >

Not To Be" about Shakespeare's hidden code, his possibly being a real gay blade, and not being the man history tells us he was. Sean Casteel gets to the bottom of the mystery.

Anyway start turning the pages, and send us over an order if you can. Postage just went up a nickle so its getting pretty darn expensive to print up copies of this newsletter and send them out. But I know a lot of you are not on the net or feel more comfortable just sending us over an order. You can use our street address for faster service:

Timothy Beckley

11 East 30th Street, 4R

NY NY 10016

Note: This issue is dedicated to my niece's husband, Ricky Sweatt, who passed away recently at sixty after a battle with cancer. He was "Mr. Personality," to the family and we will miss him dearly. When we couldn't get to the P.O. Box he would hand deliver our mail.

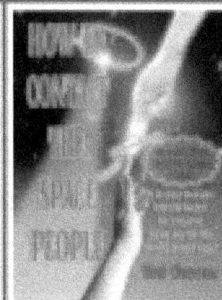

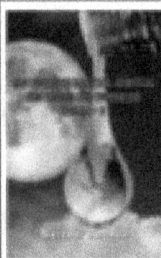

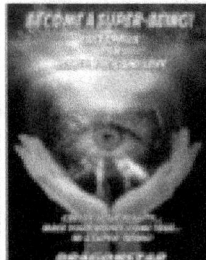

158

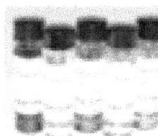

160

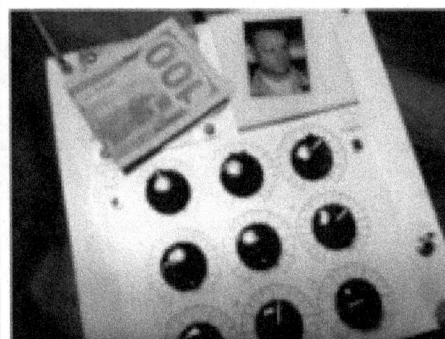

162

163

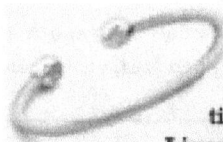

164

165

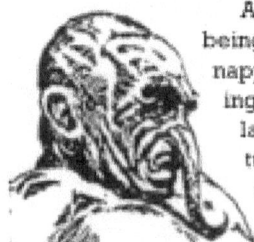

168

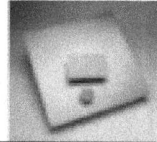

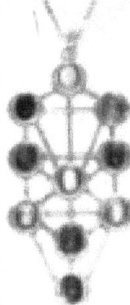

169

170

www.ingramcontent.com/pod-product-compliance
Lightning Source LLC
Chambersburg PA
CBHW081152270326

41930CB00014B/3130